P9-ECS-923

Eslen

## BILLY GRAHAM:
### is he for real?

One of Billy Graham's drawbacks, a journalist once noted, is the way he looks. In fact, he has all the physical attributes, the magnetism of a film star. He's tall, handsome, athletic—a glamour boy in every way.

The question always pops up: Is he for real?

The question has plagued him all his life. It always will . . .

Some of the most sophisticated writers of the day have tried to capture the quality of his magnetic personality in words.

The most satisfying term is "charisma" . . .

—From BILLY GRAHAM—
PROPHET OF HOPE

# Billy Graham--

## Prophet of Hope

Ronald C. Paul

903

First Church Of God
1260 West Depoy Drive
Columbia City, IN 46725

BALLANTINE BOOKS • NEW YORK

Copyright © 1978 by Ronald C. Paul

All rights reserved under International and Pan-American
Copyright Conventions. Published in the United States by
Ballantine Books, a division of Random House, Inc., New
York, and simultaneously in Canada by Ballantine Books of
Canada, Ltd., Toronto, Canada.

Library of Congress Catalog Card Number: 78-67474

ISBN 0-345-27818-6

Manufactured in the United States of America

First Edition: November 1978

# CONTENTS

# CHAPTER ONE

# Charisma

One of Billy Graham's drawbacks, a journalist once noted, is the way he looks. In fact, he has all the physical attributes, the magnetism and the charisma of a film star. He's tall, handsome, athletic—a glamour boy in every way.

The question always pops up: Is he for real?

The question has plagued him all his life. It always will. Recently a suburban woman was overheard sighing deeply as he came into a room crowded with people. The matron turned to a woman standing beside her and said:

"He's so eloquent and *so* handsome. Isn't it a shame that he isn't a politician?"

The woman she was addressing, who was Ruth Graham, Billy Graham's wife of thirty-five years, replied dryly:

"Maybe the Lord thought politics had its share and decided to give the ministry a break."

Statistically, Billy Graham stands six feet two inches tall with his shoes off. He does not put fat easily on his lean frame, and usually runs to about one hundred and eighty pounds of lanky athletic stature. His muscles do not ripple under his clothes as they might in a glamour boy's build.

In fact, during stress and strain and under the rigorous schedule of his many Crusades, he is likely to lose from ten to fifteen pounds. This loss reduces his flesh almost to the point of gauntness.

His hands are long and narrow, and his face thin.

1

His hair is a light blond that looks wind-burned and sun-bleached. His eyes are blue, deep-set and brilliant.

When seated, he tends to slouch, with his long legs stretched out in front of him. He walks with a bounce that threatens to break into a lope. When he shakes hands, he grips his counterpart's firmly and surely, with vigor and sincerity, without any evidence of muscle-moving technique.

He speaks in a definite Southern-type accent, but it is not the slow, dragged-out drawl common to the Deep South. In fact, when he is speaking on radio or television there is little trace of any accent. When he preaches he speaks in a kind of regionless American.

He can be called "Dr. Graham" without fear of contradiction. He has received at least four honorary degrees: a D.D. from King's College, Delaware, in 1948; a Doctor of Humanities degree from Bob Jones College in 1949; an LL.D. from Houghton College in 1950; and an LL.D. from Wheaton College in 1956.

To date he has participated in over two hundred Crusades for Christ. In other words, he has made over two hundred visits to specific communities in America, Europe, Asia, Africa and Australia, in an attempt to persuade people to take up Christianity, to make a "decision for Christ," as he calls it.

Over fifty million people have seen him during these Crusades. Many millions more have heard him and seen him on radio and television. Of the fifty million who have seen him, one and a half million have made their commitment to Christ, converted by Billy Graham to Christianity.

He has a radio show, *Hour of Decision,* which plays on nine hundred stations weekly. He writes a daily column, "My Answer," that is published in two hundred newspapers with a combined circulation of twenty-two million. He publishes a magazine, *Decision,* begun in 1960, which today has a circulation of over five million monthly.

In the history of the world, Billy Graham ranks as the most popular evangelist of all time.

J. Willard Marriott, a Mormon millionaire and hotel-chain head, says, "Billy Graham is a sort of itinerant preacher who represents all religions. He's the leading religious man of our time—and he is noncontroversial."

About himself, Billy Graham says, "I am a citizen of heaven."

There is more to him than just a pretty face and a fine-looking body. Some of the most sophisticated writers of the day have tried to capture the quality of his magnetic personality in words. The most satisfying term, and one currently in vogue, is "charisma."

The word "charisma" is a direct borrowing from the Greek, the root word meaning "grace," with "charisma" meaning "favor" or "gift," akin to another Greek word, *chairein*, "to rejoice." Originally "charisma" referred to the extraordinary power of healing given a Christian by the Holy Spirit for the good of the church. Recently the word has come to refer to the personal magnetism of a leader.

Whatever "charisma" means, it is a word that describes Billy Graham's effect on people but avoids saying what actually causes it.

A collection of various keynote phrases written to pin down his particular "gift" could be summed up as follows:

(1) His personal appearance, his magnetic charm, his all-American-boy image, his handsome and clean-cut look.

(2) His voice appeal, which he can control at many different levels of power: loud when he wants it loud; soft when he wants it soft; and full of conviction and fervor when he wants it to be so.

(3) His sermons, with their unstilted prose, their folksy, familiar feel, and their images studded with illustrations that hit home to most simple people.

(4) His ability to speak—in effect, to preach—from a scanty group of notes that might contain only two or three key words for an entire subject.

(5) His actor's instinct in body movements, his ability to use his hands and his stance to persuade peo-

ple to his way of thinking because his very look shows his conviction in the truths he speaks.

(6) His ability to translate the Scriptures from the traditional and ancient narrative prose and stilted injunctions into graphic, pictorial stories told in contemporary language.

(7) His humility.

(8) His belief in Jesus Christ and in the Bible.

(9) His ability to evoke in his listeners belief that mankind's problems stem from disobedience to God's laws; that God's love is constant; and that because of Jesus Christ's atoning sacrifice, man should be beholden and obey His injunctions against greed, pride and lust.

Whatever he has, he possesses an uncanny ability to handle adversity and to turn away wrath when it surfaces. He has had plenty of opportunity to do so, given the unsettled and hostile times in which he preaches.

In 1961, during his Miami Crusade, authorities at Fort Lauderdale asked him to come and help calm an unruly crowd of a thousand college students who were giving the police trouble. They booed the mayor of Fort Lauderdale and broke up a song by Anita Bryant.

Because of the publicity for Billy Graham's Miami Crusade, the students began chanting "We want Billy Graham."

One of the first things he asked the crowd was:

"What do you believe in?"

A voice yelled out, "Sex!"

That got a great laugh from the students, given Billy Graham's straitlaced outlook on life.

Billy replied, "That's important. Without it we wouldn't be here today, would we?"

The crowd roared, and from then on they were, if not with him, at least not dead set against him. He spoke to them for more than half an hour, calming them down considerably.

Later, according to John Pollock in the official biography of Billy Graham, he said, "I've never had a more attentive audience. And all I did was talk about Jesus and the answers to life's problems that can be found only in the Bible."

Again, in 1954, during the twelve-week Greater London Crusade, the British press was up in arms over his arrival in England. He had been quoted in such a fashion that his statement seemed to cast slurs on Britain's Socialist government and the Labour Party's fourteen million loyal supporters.

His audiences, however, were very large, in spite of the bad publicity.

At one of his secular appearances, at the London School of Economics, a youth suddenly appeared in one of the high windows of the hall, stripped to the waist and hanging by one arm in a simianlike pose, casually scratching his armpit with the other hand. This apelike pose set the crowd to chuckling and wondering how Billy Graham would react.

"He reminds me of my ancestors," Billy said immediately, gesturing at the window.

The crowd laughed at that.

"My ancestors, I must remind you, all came from Britain."

That brought down the house. From that moment on, they paid attention. During the Greater London Crusade he preached to overflow audiences, with over two million Britons attending. In all, thirty-eight thousand were converted to Christ.

The press continued to heckle him, even after he had arrived and proved himself to the people. He found "Cassandra," a columnist with the *Daily Mirror,* the most offensive. In real life "Cassandra" was William Connor, a brilliant if somewhat erratic writer.

After a number of these diatribes had appeared in the *Mirror,* Billy Graham offered to have a face-to-face meeting anywhere the columnist suggested. Connor slyly said that he would be willing to have a one-on-one with Billy at The Baptist's Head, a pub named after John the Baptist whom Herod had beheaded when his daughter Salome decided against him.

Connor was amused that he would be meeting an

alleged emissary of Christ "on sinner's ground." While Billy Graham sipped lemonade—he neither drinks alcohol nor smokes—the columnist drank his ale and the two chatted.

Strangely enough, the two of them became good friends after the meeting. Connor wrote with considerable surprise: "The bloke means everything he says." Later on in a column he said, "I never thought that friendliness had such a sharp cutting edge. I never thought that simplicity would cudgel us sinners so damned hard."

"Cassandra" had caught one of the strengths of Billy Graham's hold on people: simplicity. It comes from the man's humility. He has often said:

"I'm no great intellectual, and there are thousands of better preachers than I. If God should take His hands off my life, my lips would turn to clay."

Many people have asked him why, if his talents were so slim and his chances of success so small, God chose him for the ministry.

"That's the first question I'm going to ask Him when I get to heaven," Billy Graham responds.

Because of his conservative background, he is no flaming liberal who would change society tomorrow and create the perfect world by laws and acts. "Past generations blamed their problems on sin. The present generation, not having been taught about sin, blames them on society."

He has said, "Certainly, we must do all in our power to bring social justice to work for peace among nations, to put down poverty. These are proper concerns of the church.

"But even though you give people the highest standard of living, firm laws that make social and racial justice mandatory, and assign aid by the billions to needy people, your efforts will be largely futile if greed, prejudice and hatred are still there.

"God alone can remove these elements from human nature."

It is a conservative man's outlook, but also a religious man's. Billy Graham believes that the first step is to get man "right," and then let man get society "right." That is the reason he has gone into the profession he has, to show man the right way—through Christ.

"I don't know what the future holds," he once said, "but I know Who holds our future."

Although conservative, he has stood up against racism and segregation as few of his fellow Southern preachers have. Since the early 1950s he has preached to integrated audiences, in the South as well as the North.

"We should work for peace," he says, "but all we can really do is patch things up, because the real war is in man's own heart. Only when Christ comes again will the lions lie down with the lambs, and the little white children of Alabama walk hand in hand with the little black children."

Politically, his friendship with President Richard M. Nixon stirred up a great deal of controversy among partisan Democrats and Republicans and among large segments of the American public. The truth of the matter was that the two had met at Burning Tree Golf Club during a foursome back in the 1950s, when Nixon was a senator, even before he became Vice-President in Dwight D. Eisenhower's administration.

In fact, Billy knew President Nixon's parents from his Southern California Youth for Christ days. As Quakers, they had always participated in revival meetings. He had met them years before.

Yet he and Nixon had never discussed politics together.

"But on every other subject, including the importance of strong personal faith, we talk freely." According to Billy Graham, Nixon didn't mind people knowing he had deep religious convictions, although he wasn't very good at articulating them publicly.

"That comes, I think," Billy said, "from his reticent Quaker background."

During the Watergate crisis Billy Graham met several

times with Nixon in an attempt to guide him and give him spiritual advice and aid at a time when the beleaguered President needed it most.

On December 16, 1973, in fact, at the height of Watergate, he held a service for the President and Mrs. Nixon in the East Room of the White House. Senators, congressmen, military leaders and Supreme Court justices were present, along with other influential Americans.

It was the forty-second White House Worship Service under Nixon's regime, and the third one at which Billy Graham preached. Before the service the Army Chorus sang, in place of the Yale Whiffenpoofs, who were boycotting the service because of the Watergate scandals.

At the time, Nixon's two highest White House aides had just been dismissed because of Watergate-related actions. Billy Graham was under heavy pressure from the public and many of his counselors to offer a public rebuke to Nixon.

However, he refrained and instead spoke on the dark situation of the country at the time—Watergate, the Middle East war and the energy crisis were all in the news—and pointed out that worse times were ahead if repentance was not forthcoming.

Later, when his closest aides questioned him, wondering aloud why he had not castigated Nixon, he replied:

"When a friend is down, you don't go and kick him—you try to keep him up. I have personal high regard for the President. I think many of his judgments have been very poor, especially in the selection of certain people, or the people who selected others for him.

"I think there's a difference between *doing* the wrong thing and *being* wrong. For a person to err in his judgment is not wrong, or not sin.

"I also think there is a difference between judgment and integrity. I have confidence in the President's integrity—but some of his judgments have been wrong and I just don't agree with them."

The East Room service on December 16 was the last for President Nixon, who resigned his office August 9, 1974. Since that date, the evangelist has not preached in the White House at all.

For some years now Billy Graham has been such a well-known figure that he has not had time enough to take care of the business end of his ministry. For that purpose, the Billy Graham Evangelistic Association was formed in 1950. It is now staffed by five hundred people, and answers over fifty thousand letters a week. It sponsors more than two hundred Crusades a year. There are Billy Graham offices in Paris, London, Frankfurt, Sydney, Buenos Aires, Atlanta, Burbank (California) and other cities.

Billy Graham takes no direct contributions, or "love offerings," as they are called by the clergy. Nor does he take private donations or honorariums for his appearances.

He is paid a straight yearly salary of $24,500 from the proceeds of the BGEA, which also pays his principal assistants and associates.

Married to Ruth Bell Graham, whom he met while attending Wheaton College, he has five children and lives in a comfortable ten-room house on a hillside in the Blue Ridge Mountains near Montreat, on the borders of North and South Carolina.

The house was built by money supplied by ten business friends, and by the proceeds of the sale of his father's farm in Charlotte. It is a cozy place with a beautiful view and a great deal of private space around it. Billy practices golf on the lawn in the summer. Two rocking chairs, presents from Lyndon Johnson, stand nearby.

The long driveway that leads up to the house is enclosed by metal gates at the bottom. These gates are activated by a button on the dashboard of his car.

Visitors who happen to stray onto the entrance see

two signs. One announces that vicious dogs are let loose at night. The other says:

### TRESPASSERS WILL BE EATEN

He is not now generally bothered by rubberneckers or casual travelers, but at one time his small home in Montreat looked like land picked over by a swarm of locusts. Celebrity-seekers constantly stripped plants, flowers, tree limbs and souvenirs of any kind and took them away with them.

To balance out the large number of Americans who clamor for Billy Graham, who listen to his every word on radio and television, and who flock to him for succor, there are many who just can't stand the man.

His particular life-style tends to make communication with many of his fellow Americans difficult if not impossible. There are those who can't accept his enthusiasm for the "American Dream." There are others who criticize his presentation of all-American athletic types and pretty beauty-contest winners as the ordinary healthy people that all Christians aspire to be and can become. "It just ain't so," one unfriendly detractor says.

Others comment, "A salesman for Billy Graham he is, a man of God he isn't."

Many tend to think that Billy Graham's natural habitat is the plush, oak-paneled boardrooms of wealthy power-block executives, and picture him always in the country-club locker rooms of the extremely successful, discussing cash donations.

In fact, it is said that those who believe in him most do so exactly because he reflects what they themselves are: self-made men in tailored suits who have risen to the top in the belief that God rewards the righteous—didn't God reward them?

It is also true that the Billy Graham type of evangelistic approach to religion is not for everyone. Yet for those to whom it does appeal, it is a return to the old days of hymn-singing and body-swaying, of down-home spirituality at church on Sunday. It is a return to the good old days, when revival meetings were the usual thing during planting- and harvesting-time festivals.

Not all churchmen like evangelism, either. Theologians like Reinhold Niebuhr attack "the Nixon-Graham doctrine of the relation of religion to public morality" because it throws an "aura of sanctity on contemporary public policy, whether morally inferior or outrageously unjust: simply because it is the 'word of the Lord.' "

Stephen Rose points out: "It was this type of complacent conformity that the Founding Fathers feared and sought to eliminate in the First Amendment."

Actually, as the noted sociologist Robert Bellah writes, the God of civil religion, which Billy Graham espouses, is related more to law and order and right than to salvation and love. This civil God, he points out, served quite a good purpose on the frontier, where the revival tent and the camp meeting were the usual manifestations of religious celebration.

As the frontier settled down, however, this type of "religion" became centered and contained in the tiny regional churches. From there it moved over to local groups representing the law—groups like the state militia—and finally became identified with both the flag and the courts.

Billy Graham, some sociologists claim, shapes his dogma on the civil religion of Rousseau, espoused over two hundred years ago: "the existence of a mighty, intelligent and beneficent Divinity, possessed of foresight and providence, the life to come, the happiness of the just, the punishment of the wicked, the sanctity of the social contract and the laws."

Actually, Billy Graham is far more pessimistic about the future of mankind than Jean Jacques Rousseau ever was.

"I personally think we may be approaching the end of our history," he said recently. "There are about twenty-eight signs that Jesus said to watch for, and every one of them is happening: worldwide rebellion, worldwide sexual immorality, the travel increase, the tremendous knowledge explosion, the regathering of Israel to her own land. I know that the Middle East is the place where God's prophetic clock is ticking away even now. The Bible says that Armageddon will begin there."

Yet if he fears for the future, he is still able to draw people into the fold with him. The Southern Baptist Church, of which he is now the principal spokesman, is the largest religious group in the United States, with roughly twenty-five million members. Nashville, Tennessee, where its headquarters are located, is the heart and center of the hymn-singing Bible Belt.

At present the main thrust of Billy Graham's Crusades is at the youth of the country. No one is more aware of their unhappiness, their hopelessness, their lack of confidence in our form of government, than Billy Graham.

"Young people will listen with respect," he says, "even eagerness, if you talk to them straight from the shoulder."

He has been doing that since the "hippie" days of the 1960s when the new life-style came in—long hair, blue jeans and the commune life. To prove his point, he notes that three quarters of his audiences now are twenty-five years of age or under.

Those are the people of the future, the ones he wants to guide.

With the statistical average of conversions standing at a high of three and a half percent each Crusade, Billy Graham has a good chance to bring a lot of unhappy young folk into the fold of Christianity.

According to Dr. Kenneth Chafin, consultant to Billy Graham and director of evangelism for the Southern Baptist Convention's Home Mission Board, "Billy's almost an institution now. The guy has spent thirty years becoming what he is, and he has enormous power."

Whatever there is about Billy Graham that makes people follow him, it is a very real, very human and very attractive thing. Who else could accomplish what he has done in the time he has had to do it?

# CHAPTER TWO

# Conversion

William Franklin Graham was born November 7, 1918, in an upper bedroom of a two-story white frame house near Charlotte, North Carolina. The house was located on the two-hundred-acre dairy farm where his father, William Franklin Graham, Sr., had been born in a small log cabin some quarter of a century earlier.

The farm originally had been purchased by Billy's grandfather, Crook Graham, after the end of the Civil War. Crook was a veteran who fought on the Confederate side. He himself was born on the ship that brought the Graham family over from Ulster.

The farmland proved to be prosperous acreage for Crook. He was a big, strong, bearded man, who worked hard and raised a large family. It would be difficult to imagine him as Billy Graham's grandfather.

"He'd get drunk and he'd stay drunk pretty much over Sunday," one of his sons-in-law said of him. "He didn't abuse his family, but I don't hardly think he ran his farm."

He was always deep in debt, he was in constant pain from a bullet in his leg—a souvenir of the war—and he used to amuse himself shooting off fowling pieces at suitors who had the audacity to come around courting his daughters.

But the Grahams were of Scotch-Irish stock, having sailed with so many of their kind from Ulster to the New Country. They worked hard, scrimped and saved and prospered. They were basically religious people, as befit most hard-working Southerners of that time.

14

When Crook died, in 1910, he left his farm to two of his sons, William Franklin, Sr., and Clyde. Frank and Clyde bought up adjacent acres and finally had themselves a three-hundred-acre farm of rich red soil, rolling hills and wooded land—excellent for dairy farming.

Frank Graham was a lanky, tall man, six foot two, and a pretty good dairy farmer. At the age of eighteen he was converted to Scotch Presbyterianism. In those days a religious conversion was not a strange or untoward event in a man's life. Rather, it was an accepted and expected thing.

The conversion changed Frank. Shortly after this event occurred, a friend met him and noticed the obvious difference in Frank's appearance. He was more cheerful, more outgoing, more "with it," in the current phrase. The added inner glow had made him into a new man.

They began discussing Frank's new religious faith.

"Do you suppose," the friend said, "that you could help me get what you've got?"

Frank said he thought he could. He began praying for his friend right on the spot.

A preacher later said about Frank Graham: "I'd rather have Frank Graham praying for me than almost anyone I know."

The conversion opened up new horizons for Frank. He met and fell in love with a girl named Morrow Coffee, who was a graduate of Charlotte's Elizabeth College. Like him, Morrow was of Scotch-Irish ancestry, and also was the child of a Confederate soldier.

In fact, Morrow's father, Ben Coffee, had been seriously wounded during Pickett's charge, a wipeout attack which had thoroughly decimated an entire unit of Confederate forces in one of the bloodiest actions of the Civil War.

Ben came out of it with only one leg and one eye. But he was an intelligent, spirited and honest man who loved to read Scripture and literature.

Years later, when Dwight D. Eisenhower heard that

Billy Graham's grandfather had fought in Pickett's charge, he took Billy out to the Gettysburg battlefield, where the General lived, and showed him the scene.

"You're lucky your grandfather survived to be able to have a family," he told Billy.

Morrow was a very devout Presbyterian who had been trained in the Short Catechism and knew whole passages of Scripture by heart. She believed thoroughly in the power of prayer, convinced that God supplied direct and overt answers to direct prayers.

A family friend described her in those days as "a choice parcel of Southern femininity," the stilted phraseology of the time for a good-looking girl. Obviously Frank was attracted to her for her personal attributes as well as her religious ones.

What attracted her to Frank was the fact that, being the son of a prosperous landowner, he drove one of the best and biggest buggies in the area. And, also, he had been converted.

Once married, the Grahams joined the Associated Reformed Presbyterian Church (General Synod), a very conservative branch which had split off from the Associate Reformed Church in 1822. The split occurred because the Reformed members considered the Associate Reformed too liberal. The ARPC (GS) adhered to the standards of Westminster in confession, and sang Bible psalms rather than hymns during service.

Frank Graham and his wife served active careers in the local Presbyterian Church in Charlotte. In fact, Frank had secretly always nourished a desire to be a minister himself. He had waited for the call, but God had never spoken to him.

In the South it was not strange then for any man to think of religion, or to aspire to the life. Evangelism— the tent-meeting, repentance-provoking, soul-converting kind—had lost little of its past vigor. The Bible-thumping, fire-breathing, wild-eyed evangelist was alive and flourishing.

Even when Billy was born, in 1918, the South still took its religion seriously, in contrast to the other, more urban areas, which had grown philosophically sophisticated and did not.

A normal prospect for any young man to follow was the church. Parents stood behind and pushed for careers for their offspring as evangelists, missionaries or ministers.

In fact, the most painful put-down of all was to tell a boy he had no talent for preaching. A visiting minister one day sent twelve-year-old Billy Graham packing with the barbed comment: "Run along, little fellow, you'll never be a preacher."

When her son Billy was born, Morrow Graham prayed that he would be called during his lifetime to preach the Gospel. To prepare him for the calling, she supervised his Christian teaching, along with the teaching of his brother and sisters.

Frank Graham's family consisted of Billy, his brother, Melvin, and his sisters, Catherine and Jean.

As each of her children reached ten, Morrow made them memorize the questions and answers to the Short Catechism, from Number 1—"What is the chief end of Man?"—through Number 107—"What doth the conclusion of the Lord's Prayer teach us?"

And she encouraged the youngsters to take part in the "sentence prayer" of the family's daily devotions. They were also instructed to memorize Scripture verses, starting with Proverbs 3:6: "In all thy ways acknowledge Him and He shall direct thy paths."

Billy wanted to be accepted by the Lord. In his early days at school he became aware that he was different from the other boys and girls. He was naturally left-handed, but because he wanted to be like everyone else, and definitely accepted by God, he forced himself to do everything with his right hand—evidence of his struggle for approval.

To this day, he does everything right-handed. The only trace of his early habit is the wristwatch on his right wrist, rather than his left.

There were plenty of religious revivals to go to. Billy saw dozens of preachers, all of them fiery and trumpet-

ing revivalists. His father took him to see the legendary
Billy Sunday one day. Billy Graham cringed behind the
man in front of him so the preacher's piercing eyes
couldn't pick him out of the crowd to mark him as a
sinner.

His favorite evangelist was Cyclone Mack, a lean
giant of a man with long black hair, an eagle's glare and
a ravaged face that looked as if it had been lived in
for two lifetimes. Billy loved to hear the eye-popping
details flow from Cyclone Mack's lips—details of the
life of sin and corruption he led as a gangster, gambler
and murderer before he finally found redemption in
conversion to Christianity.

Like most of their neighbors, the Grahams believed
in strict parental discipline. For fidgeting and daydream-
ing during an overlong sermon in Sharon Presbyterian
Church, Billy got a whacking one Sunday from his
father's wide tough leather belt right in the middle of
the service. His mother was just as apt to go at him
with her long hickory switch if he didn't have his
catechism right.

Another time, when Billy turned up on the farm with
a cud of chewing tobacco, his father, an inveterate
tobacco-chewer himself, gave him a painful whipping
and fired the hired hand who had given it to Billy.

Again, when the sale of beer was legalized in North
Carolina at the beginning of Franklin D. Roosevelt's
first term as a liberalizing feature of his New Deal,
Frank went to town and bought two bottles. He forced
Billy and one of his sisters to drink them down straight
and quick. Billy's stomach learned its lesson. Since that
day he has never touched alcohol.

In his early years Billy wasn't all that enamored of
the religious life. In his mind he lumped undertakers
and clergymen in the same category, vowing that he
would be neither. Yet he never challenged the religious beliefs of either of his parents, unlike many
youths of today.

During his formative years Billy was involved in all
the farm chores then common to rural families. The

Grahams had twenty-five cows, which he milked at 3:00 A.M. each day. After milking them, he gathered the cans together, packed them in a truck and delivered them to four hundred customers in the Charlotte area. Then, after school was over, he would come back to the farm and spend the fading hours plowing. In the evening he would once again become involved in milking.

His life was overlaid by the theme of work. Yet in spite of its strictures, he had plenty of time for laughter, fun and the "good times" his peers had.

One of his idols was his father's Negro foreman, Reese Brown. Brown was a former Army sergeant who had fought in World War I. The veteran was a deep believer in the Christian way of life and imparted a lot of his philosophy to young Billy. In fact, it was his guidance and instruction that gave Billy his first practical appreciation of the Gospel.

According to Billy, Reese Brown was one of the straightest men he had ever known, and one of the strongest. Years later he could clearly recall Brown's capacity for work, and particularly loved the way the foreman could hold down a bull all by himself while it was being dehorned.

The teaching of the finer points of Christianity, however, was left to Billy's mother.

During his teens young Billy was very popular with his classmates at school. His thick wavy blond hair, his bright, sparkling blue eyes and his lean, tall figure made him a prime target for the eyes of the pretty girls.

And he had free use of the family car after he had finished his farm chores. With that, he could get around town to almost anywhere he wanted. Also, he was more than a fair-to-middling baseball player.

By the time he was sixteen his social activities were taking precedence over his devotions—much to his mother's concern. He indulged in moments of typical teen-age rebelliousness, and at one time characterized the devotional readings that were the habit of the Graham family as "hogwash."

It was during his sixteenth year that he underwent the same religious experience that his father had—conversion.

The word is no longer used in many churches, because in these secular days the actual fact of conversion has become unfamiliar. However, it is historically accurate to say that all the great Christian evangelists, by their own admission and testimony, underwent conversion.

On the Damascus Road, St. Paul was converted. It happened to St. Augustine in his mother's garden in Milan. During his translation of the Gospels into Greek, Erasmus was converted. And one day, reading the Scriptures, Jonathan Edwards was converted. It happened to George Whitefield during a long illness. And to John Wesley conversion occurred in Aldersgate Street, London.

It is also a fact that for every prominent Christian evangelist the conversion was an actual turning point in his life—a religious crossroads at which he was transformed from a mediocrity to a leader, from a run-of-the-mill person to a superior being, from a man on the street to a leader of men.

When it happened to Billy Graham in 1934, the country was in the midst of the Great Depression. Businesses were failing everywhere. There was no money. Jobs were scarce. Even a prosperous farmer like Frank Graham had trouble scraping together enough money to live on.

A group of thirty Charlotte businessmen decided to "revive" prosperity by the old-fashioned means of a revival meeting. The hope was that they could unite in prayer and help the community and the country out of its troubles.

Frank Graham lent one of his pastures to the group, and led them in the construction of a revival tent complete with wooden speaker's platform. And, as star attraction of the prayer meeting, he persuaded Mordecai Fowler Ham of Louisville to lead the group.

Like many of his evangelistic forebears, Ham was a

hellfire-and-brimstone preacher. He had been drummed out of the Charlotte Ministerial Association because of his insistence on exposing scandal in the ministry and attacking other ministers for their theological lapses.

In later years Ham associated himself with a group of anti-Semitic ministers, espoused far-right-wing causes and eventually faded from popularity. In 1934, however, he had the support of a lot of Christians in the South, and had been responsible for converting many of them to Christianity.

To the "tabernacle" constructed on the Graham farm —the tent and speaker's platform—Ham came to conduct his campaign for Christianity. Billy and his teenage friends visited the services for several evenings, and listened to the rousing rhetoric with a great deal of tolerant amusement at the intensity of it.

As the crowds continued to grow night by night, Billy and his friends continued to visit the revival meeting. It was a stirring sight—more than five thousand people in the place, filling every seat, on the bare-planked wooden platform, in chairs, on benches and boxes outside the tent's open walls. In the tradition of the "sawdust trail" days, the aisles were covered with sawdust to lay the mud.

The pulpit was a simple altar, unpainted and bare. Behind the altar a choir of women in white dresses and men in shirt sleeves sang in the fashion of all revival meetings before and since.

"Brother Ham" was unimpressive, however, and Billy and his friends snickered at the man's overblown prose and his thunderous oratory.

"You're a sinner," Brother Ham cried out time after time, pointing to individuals in the tent. Billy found himself trying to shrink out of sight, even though he was grinning as he went down.

Yet if Brother Ham's rhetoric didn't grab Billy, the things he said did. He was a Bible-quoter, and his quotations described the alternatives a man could choose: heaven or hell.

Mostly Billy remembered a sermon preached on John 3:16:

"For God so loved the world that He gave His only begotten Son, that whosoever believeth in Him should not perish, but have everlasting life."

Brother Ham might be a joke, but the Bible and what it said wasn't.

The very next night Billy went to the tent with Grady Wilson, his best friend, and the two of them sat in the choir, where they would be behind Brother Ham and not out in front of those blazing, fanatical eyes.

The fire-breathing evangelist began his sermon that night with the admonitory words:

"There's a great sinner in this place tonight!"

Billy's first reaction was to think to himself: "Mother's been telling him about me!"

As all evangelists did, every night Brother Ham concluded his sermon with the "altar call," inviting anyone who felt the need to join the crusade with Christ to come forward and make himself known to God.

That night when Ham gave the call, Billy hesitated. Then, abruptly, turning to Grady Wilson, he said resignedly, "Let's go."

He climbed down out of the choir box and went over to the makeshift altar. Grady was right behind him, puzzled and surprised but quite willing.

It was at that moment that Billy Graham made his decision for Christ. "It was as simple as that," he said later, "and as conclusive."

Discussing his conversion, Billy said: "There were no tears, no blazing voices, no gift of tongues." Thinking about it later, he wrote: "Have you ever been outdoors on a dark day when the sun suddenly bursts through the clouds? Deep inside, that's how I felt. The next day, I'm sure, I looked the same. But to me everything —even the flowers and the leaves on the trees—looked different. I was finding out for the first time the sweetness and joy of God, of being truly born again."

From that moment on, Billy Graham was committed to a new direction in life.

To Billy his conversion might have been a rather "simple" thing, but to his parents it was not. To them it was a complete breakthrough to God.

When Billy moved forward as a convert in the tabernacle, his father rushed across from the opposite side of the tent and threw his arms around his son, offering up his own thanks to God for showing Billy the way.

On the walk home that night, Billy Graham and Grady Wilson made a pact. Having gone so far, they said, and finding it so good, they would to the best of their ability and with God's help "go all out" for Jesus Christ.

Later Billy found the text in the Bible which would serve the two of them well and help them keep their pact:

"Being confident of this very thing, that He which hath begun a good work in you will perform it, until the day of Jesus Christ." (Philippians 1:6.)

First Church Of God
1200 West Dapoy Drive
Columbia City, IN 46725

# CHAPTER THREE

# Bob Jones

Billy Graham's religious conversion to Christ in 1934 did not result in any quick decision to take up preaching on the sawdust trail. In his biography of Billy Graham, Stanley High wrote: "He was, in fact, slow to make up his mind—not slow by what is ordinarily expected of a seventeen-year-old, but slow when one considers what extraordinary expectations were centered in him."

Frank Graham, who had never received the longed-for call to preach, was elated at his son's conversion. Frank's talents obviously lay in other fields, and he eventually came to believe that his own part in the larger plan was to raise a son who would become a preacher.

Billy's mother had a more practical reaction. Shortly after his conversion, she set aside a period every day for prayer devoted only to Billy and to the calling she believed was to be his.

In fact, she continued her prayers for seven years, ceasing them only when she was certain that Billy was well on his way to being a preacher.

Grady Wilson reacted to his conversion to Christ in a characteristically different fashion from Billy. He decided quickly that it was his destiny to preach, starting immediately. He did so every chance he got. Billy and his friends used to listen to Grady. Billy really didn't think much of his best friend's efforts.

Grady Wilson modeled himself closely on the style of Mordecai Ham, both in platform address and in theology. Like Ham and the fire-eating arm-wavers, Grady tended to be carried away by the sound of his own voice.

Stanley High wrote: "On one memorable night—when he borrowed Billy's watch and wound it, as he preached, until the stem broke—he spoke on 'God's Four Questions,' taking a full hour on questions One and Two and, by dint of considerable telescoping, half an hour on Three and Four."

It was all too much for Billy.

Grady was determined to be a success at preaching, even though his friends kept telling him that it didn't really seem to be his thing.

As for Billy, he wasn't ready for preaching yet. He really didn't know what he wanted to do. He knew for a fact what he *didn't* want to do, and that was to get up every morning at three o'clock and milk cows.

To avoid being stuck with farm chores, he had to do something useful with his time. And something "useful" in those days meant something that would bring in a little money.

He persuaded the Wilson brothers—Grady and T. W. —to attend a two-hour indoctrination course and make a two-day trial run selling Fuller Brushes door to door. They succeeded, and spent the summer as Fuller Brush salesmen.

Billy took to the job with his usual zest. He had a pleasant and engaging personality. That, combined with his clean-cut good looks, made him perfect for the job. When the average housewife saw him coming, she didn't mind one bit listening to his spiel.

"I was naturally sort of a shy fellow," Billy said later, "and I didn't particularly like to meet people. Selling brushes got me over that. It allowed me to talk with people and to sell people.

"I never took a speech course in my life. I never read a book on speech. The way I speak in the pulpit is my natural form of speaking, except that before a big crowd, I speak a bit louder."

Billy threw himself into the job of salesman. He

started every day's round with prayer, and prayed as he went from house to house and customer to customer. In addition, he worked early and late, and quite soon beat out the Wilson brothers in total sales.

Whatever it was—inherent personality, natural ability as a salesman or simply charisma—Billy wound up the summer selling more brushes than any other salesman in North Carolina, including the district manager.

After his successful summer, Billy went back to finish up his last year of high school. He was a pretty good baseball player, and he helped put the team in a top spot. His studies were mediocre, as usual, but he didn't actually disgrace himself.

Once Billy graduated, a decision had to be made as to his future. The decision came down to which of two courses to pursue: baseball or the church?

Billy was good enough to play first base for a semi-professional team in Sharon. His batting average was .275, and he was a good fielder. The first summer out of high school he made ten to fifteen dollars a game—not bad money for those Depression days.

He had been high on baseball ever since that day in grammar school when the great Babe Ruth, on a visit to Charlotte, had personally shaken Billy's hand and said:

"You could be a first baseman. You certainly do have the build for it."

Now, in 1935, what kept him from going all out for baseball was the financial situation of the team. Money was scarce, and the games were few and far between.

In the Graham household both parents were hoping that Billy would eventually forgo the rather frivolous and dubious benefits of the sports life and choose to become a man of the cloth. And because they were both Presbyterians, they believed firmly in a college education for anyone who wanted to join the clergy.

Money was hard to come by in those dark days. College was only for the well-to-do, or for those equipped psychologically and spiritually to work their way through.

Also, the Grahams were basically conservative people in a religious sense—fundamentalists, in fact. (In general terms, a fundamentalist believes in the exact word of the Bible rather than a loose interpretation of the Bible's meanings.) They did not like to think what would happen if their son was educated in an institution of learning outside the fundamentalist fold.

At that time, one of the best-known of the American fundamentalist colleges was Bob Jones College in Cleveland, Tennessee. Also, it was comparatively inexpensive. The Grahams chose it for Billy for both those reasons.

The school, founded in 1927 near Lynn Haven, on the Alabama-Florida border, specialized in training ministers, missionaries, evangelists and Christian workers generally. Even for its time it was a very straitlaced and strict school.

Neither smoking nor drinking was allowed anywhere on campus. Boys and girls were to keep their bodies at least six inches apart. Hollywood films were banned, as were cards, dancing and jazz music. Students were required to report violations of any rules or face dismissal for being disloyal.

The founder, Bob Jones, Sr., was a onetime itinerant evangelist. A colorful hellfire-and-brimstone revivalist, Jones started preaching at the tender age of nine over the backs of a mule team as he plowed his father's Alabama farm. At thirteen he held his first revival meeting. Two years later he was licensed to preach.

Shortly after he had founded his college in Lynn Haven he came out during the 1928 Presidential campaign against Governor Al Smith, the Democratic candidate. "Catholics," Jones said, "believe that children of non-Catholic parents are illegitimate. I'd rather see a nigger in the White House than Mr. Smith."

In 1933 the college moved to Cleveland, and fourteen years later transferred to Greenville, South Carolina.

A stern right-wing upholder of law and order—and the word of the Bible—Dr. Jones backed up his stringent rules and regulations with a disciplinary code, and an army of monitors—locally called the "Gestapo"— brooked no deviation.

In the words of Billy Graham's biographer, John Pollock, "Dr. Jones knew exactly what was true and false in faith, ethics and academies. He often stated publicly that his institution had never been wrong. Independent thought was so discouraged that many alumni say in retrospect that there was thought control."

Curtis Mitchell in *Billy Graham: The Making of a Crusader* (Chilton Books, 1966) wrote:

> Billy began to feel increasingly uncomfortable. On campus you were not permitted to speak to girls except during certain hours. You were not allowed to loiter. You could not leave the campus unless you signed a book.
>
> Upper classmen might have cars, but they could not drive them on Sunday. Violations were mysteriously reported and demerits awarded. If you got so many more, you were shipped home in disgrace.
>
> Another trouble galled him. The Bible was used to settle every dispute. It was the ultimate authority. Billy had always accepted the supremacy of the Bible and he had no wish to change now, but insistence on the precise meaning advanced by the school became a heavy cross. One day he violated a rule by crying: "Don't we ever have the right to figure things out for ourselves?"

In spite of his dissatisfaction with the school, he preached his first sermon during his semester at Bob Jones College. It was in a small Tennessee town nearby, the date having been arranged by Billy's roommate, Wendell Phillips. Phillips, a graduate of the Moody Bible Institute in Chicago, had been paired off with Billy in the role of a kind of big brother.

The two of them went to the church on foot, since the school's rules forbade the use of a car. It was an eleven-mile walk.

Billy's first sermon was titled "If Christ Had Not Come, What?"

Wendell Phillips later described what happened:

Billy started in the easy, casual way he always uses, but suddenly as he went along I realized I had heard this sermon before, or at least had read it. A few weeks earlier I had sold some Moody colportage books to several of the students and here, before my eyes, was one of these sermons coming to life.

Billy went right down the line in the outline and sermon and did a terrific job. But in his desire to be dramatic he gave me an awful scare.

He stood in that pulpit and declared as forcefully as he knew, "The coming of Christ was foretold centuries before the Messiah came, by type, by symbol, and by prophecy. The smoke from every Jewish altar was an index finger pointing to the Lamb of God who would take away the sins of the world. One thousand years rolled by and still no Messiah. Two thousand years and still no Christ. . . . Three thousand . . . Five thousand. . . ."

Right there I began shaking my head from my front row seat. He saw me, looked a bit perplexed, and quickly switched to another thought. After the meeting he said to me, "Wendell, why did you shake your head like that?"

I told him, "Billy, I was afraid you wouldn't stop, as you rolled the centuries back, short of fifteen to twenty thousand years, and those dear Bible-loving people—who put 6000 B.C. or so as the date of Creation—would never invite us back again."

Billy's unfamiliarity with the regimented life at Bob Jones College involved him in an episode or two that marked him as a "problem" student. Even though he eloquently talked his way out of each of these little scrapes, he left at the end of the first semester to enroll in Florida Bible Institute.

Actually, he had suffered several bad bouts of in-

fluenza in Tennessee, and may have been advised not
only by his physician but by his parents as well to move
to a different climate.

Not only that, but his roommate, Wendell Phillips,
had gone on ahead and sent back word that convinced
Billy.

"I told him," Phillips wrote later, "that his decision
was a matter for serious prayer: that schools were not
the primary thing, but that knowing God's will was of
the utmost importance. In every letter I referred him to
Proverbs 16:9: 'A man's heart deviseth his way: but
the Lord directeth his steps.'"

When Dr. Jones heard of Billy's decision to leave,
he blew up. "Billy, if you leave and throw your life
away at a little country Bible school, the chances are
you'll never be heard of. At the best, all you could
amount to would be a poor country Baptist preacher
somewhere out in the sticks."

Dr. Jones then told him: "If you're a misfit at Bob
Jones College, you'll be a misfit wherever you go."

Thirty-two years later, upon the death of Bob Jones,
Sr., his son, Bob Jones, Jr., then running the school,
sent a telegram to Billy Graham saying that neither he
nor his personal representative would be welcome at
the funeral.

# CHAPTER FOUR

# Tampa

For his second semester at college, Billy Graham enrolled at the tiny Florida Bible Institute, located a few miles outside of Tampa. Subsequently, Florida Bible Institute was renamed Trinity College and moved to Clearwater.

When Billy enrolled, the school was housed in a one-time country club called Temple Terrace, part of which had been rebuilt to accommodate the handful of students that made up its student body.

There were seventy-five of them when Billy enrolled.

Adhering to Depression tradition, most of the students worked their way partially or wholly through school. To help them out, the college ran the other half of the school as a resort hotel. The students were allowed to pay their way by working as waiters, busboys and bellhops for the tourists who stayed at the hotel.

The school was surrounded by a beautiful championship golf course. Billy did a lot of caddying at anywhere from twenty-five cents to a dollar for eighteen holes. In off moments he learned to play the game himself, a sport he still likes to follow.

His school job was dishwashing, at which he worked five hours a day at twenty cents an hour. The money he earned at the sink covered his dollar-a-day room and board. He recalled that he was the fastest and probably the best washer in the school.

"With near-boiling water, plenty of suds, I'd send

an armful of dishes through with little more than one swish."

He was so fast he kept five dryers going.

There were other jobs as well. On one occasion he took a station wagon full of tourists into Tampa for a look at the city.

"I drove those tourists into Tampa, spent the afternoon explaining the virtues of Tampa, which I didn't know anything about, and brought them back, and they all seemed happy!"

Billy liked particularly the climate of Tampa. It was warm and mild compared to Tennessee, where he had always been subject to bouts of the flu.

The college was not a seminary, nor did it have either a liberal arts or letters-and-science curriculum. It was headed by Dr. William T. Watson, minister of a Christian and Missionary Alliance church in Tampa.

Teaching was done by preachers, aided by visiting ministers and evangelists. The doctrines of the school were Biblical fundamentalist.

However, the Biblical fundamentalism at Florida Bible Institute was not a strict one. For that time and place it was quite a liberal and tolerant version. Some of the preachers were Methodists and Presbyterians. Dissenting points of view were given a fair and friendly hearing.

Actually, the school was a little ahead of its time. There was a great deal of emphasis on Christian social service, in addition to the Gospel. Basically, and for all practical purposes, the main purpose of the college was to encourage its students to think.

And yet the Bible was the most indispensable textbook at the school. A personal religious experience—conversion—was looked on as the first and most important element of a Christian's credentials. Ambition for full-time Christian service was the aim of every student.

There were girl students at Florida Bible Institute as well as boys. There was one whom Billy met who was as devout as she was pretty. Billy had always been popular with the girls back in Charlotte, and he was popular with the girls in Tampa as well.

He decided that Emily Regina Cavanaugh was the right one for him, and Emily decided that he was the right one for her. It happened quickly, during that first semester, and by the end of the first few months of their acquaintance they were as good as engaged. Stanley High wrote:

> Finally, to put something of an official seal on it, Billy—when the time of the annual class party came around—instead of sending her the twenty-five-cent corsage customary for such occasions, went all-out and bought her one for fifty cents.
>
> It was love's lucre lost. She never wore it. Without warning, but with a highly feminine sense of timing, she used this occasion to tell Billy she had thrown him over for another.

The trouble was, she said, Billy had never really been religious enough for her. He seemed to be a parvenu, a dilettante at the Gospel. He was not serious about Christianity. Even though he espoused Christ, he went about it with a lackadaisical attitude. He was an irresponsible person.

She told him quite frankly that he wouldn't get very far or be very important in the church. She then told him that one of his best friends, Charles Massey, a senior, had everything Billy lacked. He did well in school. He had plans to go on to theological school. He was going to be a preacher. She told Billy she had decided on Charles rather than on Billy.

That was it for Billy. He didn't fight back—he couldn't. It was all decided by the girl, not by him. Wendell Phillips was home on sick leave. Billy wrote him an impassioned note:

"All the stars have fallen out of my sky. There is nothing to live for. We have broken up."

Wendell reached for his Bible and found an apt quotation.

"Read Romans 8:28," he wrote to Billy. " 'And we know that all things work together for good to them that love God, to them who are the called according to His purpose.' "

Not a bad letter, in fact. Billy read it and thought about it. He had been wandering about the environs of the country club in his emotional desolation. Now he went out there again and looked at the grass and the trees and the stars.

Shortly afterward he wrote back to Wendell.

"I have settled it once and for all with the Lord. No girl or friend or anything shall ever come first in my life. I have resolved that the Lord Jesus Christ shall have all of me. I care not what the future holds. I have determined to follow Him at all cost."

He wasn't kidding. He concentrated more on his studies, and particularly tried to improve his oratory for his preaching class. Although the course was usually accomplished by the average student with a couple of sermon outlines from which he would elucidate ad lib, Billy opted for a more difficult course.

He began writing his sermons in full and then reading them aloud, listening to the way they sounded. Naturally, he could not rehearse in front of other people, so he took to wandering out into the remote wooded areas of the campus near the Hillsborough River. There, hidden behind the trees, he preached to the alligators and other swamp animals.

"If there were no kind words from the audience, neither was there any criticism," he later said.

Composing sermons occupied most of his study time. When he saw one he liked, he copied it out with his own personal adaptations and preached it, changing it when it sounded wrong.

When preachers came to the school to lecture, he would take notes on their pulpit mannerisms and try them out, gesture by gesture, schtick by schtick. Those he liked he kept. Those he disliked he threw out or modified to fit his own needs.

"Many times," he recalled, "surrounded by darkness,

I called out from that cypress stump and asked sinners to come forward and accept Christ. There were none to come, of course. But as I waited I seemed to hear a voice within me saying, 'One day there will be many.' "

As he gained facility in preaching Billy began to be more critical of his own efforts. There was something wrong, he knew. He could feel that it was not right. However, at the same time he began to like his style, too. The conflict led him to all kinds of self-doubts and insecurities.

One night after he had preached a particularly moving swamp sermon, he realized he was being almost emotionally affected by his own call to Jesus Christ. He wandered over to the Temple Terrace golf course, where, somewhere near the eighteenth hole, he had held earlier dialogues with himself and with God.

There he "argued with the Lord," as he phrased it, sometimes out loud. He appealed for advice. "I can't ever be a good preacher," he said. "I don't want to do it. No church would have me."

And finally, Billy related years afterward, "God talked right back: 'I can use you. I need you. You make the choice, I will find the place.' "

About midnight, Billy finished his dialogue. "All right, Lord," he said, "if You want me You have got me."

He wrote his parents:

"Dear Mother and Dad: I feel that God has called me to be a preacher."

From that moment on, his whole life took on a sense of urgency. Billy Graham became a man in a hurry. Immersed in the religious life, he got down to business and preached even more to the tree stumps along the Hillsboro River.

It was at this point that help came to Billy from an outside source.

The Reverend John R. Minder, Dean of the Institute, taught the course in preaching in which Billy was enrolled. He was a straight-from-the-shoulder fundamentalist who preached with total authority. The source of his authority was the Bible.

Dean Minder was an inspiration to the students, and particularly to Billy. Young Billy was too honest with himself and with God to treat lightly a thing as important as a divine call. He realized that if he took the call he would have to subordinate all his ambitions and his endeavors to the religious life.

When he finally made his decision, he began to study Dean Minder's methods. The Dean had a simple, three-part approach to the preparation of a sermon:

(1) Know your subject.
(2) Believe your message.
(3) Speak it with conviction.

"Not knowing your subject," he said, "is the source of half-baked sermons: sermons which, like Ephraim, are 'a cake not turned.'

"Believing it halfway or in part with reservations may be the way to produce an essay; it's no way to produce a sermon.

"And if there's no fire in the preacher, there's likely to be none kindled in the people."

Those are the three key tenets of sermon-writing that Billy Graham has always clung to. He got more from Dean Minder than those three points. It was his Christian life, his kindliness, his patience, his availability when things went wrong, at all hours of the day or night, that gave Billy the lift he needed during those crucial years of his life.

Having heard of Billy's solitary preaching in the swamp, Dean Minder began to look around for a church that might give Billy a real pulpit from which to speak.

One Sunday he took Billy with him to visit a Baptist church not far from Palatka, Florida. The minister there asked the Dean to preach for him that evening.

"No," said Dean Minder.

The minister was surprised. "No?"

"Billy Graham will be preaching here tonight."

The minister nodded.

Billy was scared witless. "You don't understand! I've never really preached in my life!"

"That," said Dean Minder, "is what we are about to remedy. If you run out of anything to say before the time is up, I'll take over."

For Dean Minder's course, Billy had prepared four sermons and memorized and practiced them until he had them letter-perfect. Now he got up during the service, began the sermons and found to his horror that he had exhausted his entire repertoire within ten minutes.

At that point, however, instead of surrendering the pulpit to Dean Minder, he began adding proved testimony he had witnessed himself, and kept going for all the allotted time.

When he had finished, he asked if there were any present who wanted to accept Christ as Savior. Several of the congregation raised their hands. Billy asked them to come forward for prayer. Dean Minder wrote:

> One rough-handed woodsman who had raised his hand did not move. Billy left the pulpit and went down to talk with him. As Billy approached, the man said loudly,
> "You don't need to think because you go to that school down there that you know everything."
> Billy, surprised and embarrassed, backed away without replying. But that man and Billy's inability to say the right word troubled him for days.

Dean Minder soon pointed out to Billy that perhaps God was taking him down just a bit, after he had preached with such authority, giving Billy a lesson in the sin of pride.

After that Billy preached often: in trailer camps, in churches, at rescue missions in Tampa, on street corners.

Once he stood in front of a Tampa saloon, preaching to people standing at the bar. The bartender told him to get out, but Billy wouldn't go. Finally the bartender shoved him out and ordered him to stay away. He wouldn't leave. The bartender once again pushed him away.

Staggering to his feet, Billy realized his clothes were dirty and torn. He was angry at the bartender, but then he stopped.

"I remembered the words of Jesus," he said later, "and felt that I was suffering for Christ's sake. It was quite pointless, the way I went about it, all zeal and no knowledge, but those were experiences that helped me develop."

When he preached at Palatka again, he was paid $2.25 for the sermon. He was in a quandary about what to do with the money. To him, teaching the word of the Lord was not to be equated with cash.

Dean Minder told him that to labor in God's vineyard was to be supported by the people of God.

About his style of speaking, biographer John Pollock wrote, "He preached too loud. He preached too fast. He dramatized and was dubbed by some 'the preaching windmill.' "

Dean Minder asked Billy to take his place at the pulpit of his Tampa church for six weeks at six dollars a Sunday. Billy did so, concluding each sermon with an altar call. Word got around that the "boy preacher from North Carolina" was starting up a miniature revival.

After that, he and the Dean conducted a revival campaign in Palatka. At the end of the first week's meeting, the Dean drew Billy aside.

"These people don't want to hear me. They're coming to hear you. You stay while I go back to the school. Let's see what you do on your own."

The church at Palatka was Southern Baptist. Billy was Presbyterian. To the Baptists who listened to him, there was one thing that was wrong with Billy: He had never been baptized—that is, immersed.

The rumor spread that "the boy preacher" wasn't even baptized. It was a damning report. Billy looked into his own heart and studied the situation.

From the pulpit that night he confirmed the rumor: He had not been baptized. But at the end of the meeting—along with the revival's converts—he would be.

With them he went to a nearby lake, and there he became baptized.

"It was a glorious experience," he later recalled. It was in the same church at the end of the revival period that he converted to Baptism, and later—with the converts of the revival as his credentials—was ordained to preach by the St. John's Baptist Association of Northern Florida.

After Palatka, he preached regularly in a trailer park at the Tampa Gospel Tabernacle. He was a forceful, sincere speaker, with a straight presentation of what he called God's Good News.

He had begun to get the feel of evangelism at Palatka. Now, instead of a career as a preacher, he began to think he might make a better evangelist. From his Fuller Brush labors he knew that he had all the right instincts for salesmanship. Could that instinct and ability be used to sell the word of God to disbelievers?

During his final year at college Billy got in a lot of long walking—usually several miles a day. He used it both for exercise and for devotion. As he walked along, he prayed. He prayed that God would make good use of his life.

In 1940 he graduated from the Florida Bible Institute. The entry under his picture read:

"Billy Frank Graham, Charlotte, N. C. Activities: President, Senior Class; Assistant Pastor; Chaplain; Tampa Trailer Court; Volley Ball, Swimming. Personal Aim: Evangelist. Favorite Song: Faith of Our Fathers. Favorite Scripture Verse: Jude 3: 'I exhort you that ye should earnestly contend for the faith which was once delivered unto the saints.' "

# CHAPTER FIVE

# Wheaton

When Billy Graham returned to his home town after graduation, he found that news of his accomplishments as the "boy preacher" of Tampa had preceded him. In fact, he found a number of invitations from nearby communities to conduct revivals there.

He accepted one of them in York, Pennsylvania, and in the following summer conducted his own first revival meeting.

Things were looking up for him. He had become a member of a large church group—the Southern Baptists were then and are today the largest single denomination of Protestant sects in the country—and he was good at his job and recognized as such by parishioners and professionals alike.

At the time there was a great deal of tension in the country over the possibility of war. The ministry usually becomes very important during times of stress. Billy Graham would never have to look very far for a job.

Had he become an evangelist at that point, modeled after the evangelists he had already seen—Mordecai Ham and Bob Jones, Sr.—he would probably have gone on to a successful career in that field.

No matter how good a field it was, it would have been a limited one. He would have traveled about the small towns in the South, pitched his tents, launched fire-eating attacks on sin and tried to save sinners throughout the fundamentalist South.

There was more for him. His parents were the first to realize that. And both of them still had good reason to believe education would be the making of their eldest son.

Although they knew he had got a decent college education already, they also knew that he needed more— a good theological background to round out his Bible studies.

Next fall he enrolled at Wheaton College, a respected coeducational evangelist school in Illinois, not far from Chicago. His mother approved of it most highly. It was a reputable school with very high academic standards.

Billy learned to his sorrow that most of his work at Florida Bible Institute could not be transferred for credit at Wheaton. But they did allow him enough for about one year's study. This meant that he had three more years to go at Wheaton. He chose to major in anthropology.

The college was founded by pioneers who had come from New England to Illinois by covered wagon, oxcart and boat. They were pious people who worked hard and believed in God. Wherever they went they planted Christian colleges to train their offspring.

They used the savings they put away from solid hard work, and they used the faith they had been brought up with, and they put them together to make the miracles they felt necessary in the building of a successful frontier. Colleges and schools were manifestations of these miracles.

Wheaton College was founded in 1853 by Wesleyan Methodists. Even at that time it was a nondenominational college. Today its leaning is probably more Presbyterian than Methodist.

Springing from a one-story limestone schoolhouse, it has a thirty-five-acre campus today with a student body of sixteen hundred. Its academic rating is in the top bracket of American colleges.

Each semester at Wheaton starts with a week's evangelistic services. Each day classes begin with a prayer. There is a daily devotional chapel hour for all students.

Campus revivals are not uncommon. Numerous voluntary prayer groups are held during the week. The highest honor a student can achieve is election to the presidency of the Christian Council.

Wheaton graduates number more than a thousand foreign missionaries serving today in eighty-eight countries around the world.

When Billy Graham arrived there he was, not surprisingly, short of cash. The Grahams believed that their children should earn the greater part of their way through college.

He got a job driving a truck, and did work for the building and grounds department of the college. By scrimping and saving his money, he was soon able to buy the truck. He then set himself up in the hauling business.

The tall, blond and handsome Southerner became a much-noticed man on campus. By this time he had learned to dress in a spick-and-span, flashy way.

He was older than most of the other students, having already spent four years in college in Tampa. Not only that, word of his preaching ability had preceded him to Wheaton. He was definitely a man in a class by himself.

Also, he seldom turned down a chance to talk about or practice preaching. He used his third-floor room for speaking. He preached whenever he had time, often at odd hours of the night.

In the preparation of his sermons, Billy used every method he could think of. One of his roommates, Jimmy Johnson, wrote later how he had been routed out of bed by Billy one night.

"Jimmy," Billy told him, "I've got to preach tomorrow night. You've got to help me get an outline."

Jimmy got out his Bible.

"Then, the next night," Jimmy recalled, "I went down and heard him preach that outline. He did such a tremendous job I sat there and took notes on my own sermon."

Billy's preaching fees began to increase. Finally he was able to cover his living expenses. At that point he closed out his trucking business.

In his junior year Billy was asked to take over as pastor of the Wheaton Student Church. The post had been held by Dr. V. Raymond Edman, later president of Wheaton.

Things were happening to Billy Graham at Wheaton that were widening his horizons considerably. No longer was he bound in by the strict borders of the Bible. It was not that his beliefs were watered down, nor was it that his beliefs were distorted. It was simply that wider vistas were opened to him.

At Wheaton it was not a virtue to cling to the narrowness of Christianity, nor to the confines even of the Bible as it was written.

The concept was held by those in charge at Wheaton that God could find ways to make use of many people whose religious life-style was not exactly like everyone else's.

Wheaton did not undermine in any way the authority of Billy's preaching. Far from it—it gave him *more* authority. And its tone and content were quite a bit less in the tradition of Jonathan Edwards' "Sinners in the Hands of an Angry God" and more in the tradition of John Wesley.

In other words, hellfire and damnation were used more rarely in Billy's sermons after he came to Wheaton, and now were never used in his altar calls. At Wheaton Billy found that God's foremost attribute was love, not the raising of fear.

One of those who helped Billy to see Christian life in a new setting at Wheaton was Professor Mortimer Lane. He helped open the doors and windows of Billy's orthodoxy to new sights and sounds.

Soon Billy got a chance to preach as part-time pastor of the United Gospel Tabernacle, where both students and professors worshipped. Things were opening up for him.

A much more personal thing happened that had lasting consequences for Billy while he was at Wheaton. He met Ruth McCue Bell.

Billy had heard of her even before he saw her. One

of his classmates told him that one of the most beautiful coeds at Wheaton was also the most devout.

The informant pointed out that she got up every
morning at five o'clock and spent two hours before
breakfast and classes in Scripture reading and prayer.

Billy wasn't long in meeting her. He was working
one morning moving furniture into a rooming house.
His truck was backed up to the sidewalk and he was
fighting a big overstuffed chair, trying to get it up the
front steps to the porch. Grimy and sweating, he looked
up to see her waiting to go into the house, where she
lived.

Later he recalled that she was so cool and comfortable in a dainty white dress that it was exasperating.
"But she was a vision if I ever saw one."

Ruth McCue Bell was a trim five foot five, with
brown eyes, black hair modishly set and facial lines
that were soft and clean. She wore smart clothes.

Reared in a home that was as traditionally dedicated
to religion as Billy's, she considered the family enclave
a place where possession of the faith was elemental.

Her parents, Dr. and Mrs. L. Nelson Bell, had been
medical missionaries of the Presbyterian Church in
China. Ruth was born in June 1920 in the mission compound at Tsing Kiang Pu, where her father was sta-
tioned. Tsing Kiang Pu is a Kiangsu Province city about
three hundred miles north of Shanghai. After his arrival
there in 1916, Dr. Bell directed the building and was
subsequently in charge of the 380-bed mission hospital
there.

Ruth and her two sisters were brought up in the
mission. She learned to speak Chinese before she could
speak English. Her mother took charge of her education
through the grammar-school grades. It was a terrifying,
hair-raising kind of life for the young girl.

She and her two sisters could never leave the mission
compound without an adult guard for fear of being
kidnapped and held for ransom by the roving bandits
who plundered the area.

As they walked about outside the compound they

frequently saw the bodies of Chinese babies who had been left to die on the roadside by parents unable to feed them.

Danger was never far off. It was rare that they went to sleep without the constant sound of gunfire somewhere in the distance ringing in their ears.

When she was old enough for high school, her parents sent her away to a school for missionary children in Korea.

Her first Christmas away from home was a desperately unhappy one for her. She wrote to her parents saying that she had prayed about it and God had told her that going home for Christmas was His will for her.

Her mother wrote back: "You say God is leading you to come home. We say that as long as we are responsible for you, He is going to lead *us* as to what to do for you. Neither your father nor I feel He is leading us to bring you back to China for Christmas."

She stayed in Korea for the holidays.

In 1941 the Japanese and Communist invasions occurred simultaneously, driving the Bells from the country.

The Bells were luckily able to escape to America, where they settled in Montreat, North Carolina. Dr. Bell established a successful surgical practice in nearby Asheville.

Montreat was a quaint little hamlet in the rural section of North Carolina. It had become a town favored by retired missionaries and pastors of the Presbyterian faith.

The environment was strict and almost spartan. The church dominated the lives of everyone there. Ruth found little else to do but go to church conferences, to church, and for walks by the church college.

She decided finally to try for Wheaton College, and when she was accepted her sister Rosa enrolled there, too.

By the time she was a college coed, Ruth had made up her mind as to her future. She had committed her life to the Lord as a young girl, in China. She was planning to return to Asia as a missionary. The area she had chosen for her work was the remotest spot in the civilized world—Tibet.

If her parents were unable to give their three daughters advice as to the men they should marry, they made up for the lack in constant prayer. The girls, in their choosing, took into account not only the man but also his relationship to God.

It was not surprising, knowing Ruth Bell's early training and dedication to God, that her first date with Billy was to a Sunday afternoon of sacred music—Handel's *Messiah*—at the Wheaton College chapel. After it was over they took a long walk home.

She said later: "I knew then that here was a man who knew where he was going: He was going ahead with God. I knew he had one purpose: to please God, regardless." That night she prayed: "Oh, Lord, if you'll give me the privilege of sharing my life with this man, I could have no greater joy."

There was, however, one obstacle she had overlooked: her own plans for a life as a missionary in Tibet. Ruth decided she needed to consult with Rosa.

"If God got me here to Wheaton in spite of the war, and if He's provided the money and if He's helped me through my courses—then hasn't He been leading me straight back to the mission field?" Ruth wanted to know.

Rosa thought about that a moment. "But did you ever think that He might have led you here to meet Billy? Maybe God does want you over there in Tibet as an old-maid missionary, but I doubt it. I think He wants you right here in this country—as Billy Graham's wife."

Another problem loomed. It was Billy. "I was as sure as she was," he said later. "But she knew what a suitor ought to be and do, and I didn't."

Ruth consulted with her sister again. "He's being cautious," she told Rosa. "Now you know that's no way to court a girl. Maybe he doesn't care."

Rosa decided to go for broke. She suggested that Ruth have a date or two with someone else.

She did.

It worked.

As soon as he learned of Ruth's other personal interests, he confronted her with an ultimatum: Either she could date him and no one else, or she could date the lot and forget all about him.

There was yet another complication, at least in part. Ruth Bell had never been converted to Christianity; she had simply grown into it. That didn't conform to the strictest precepts of the fundamentalism with which Billy had been brought up.

Salvation to a fundamentalist involved rebirth. Being born again required a definite crossing over—usually accompanied by a strong emotional upsurge—at a specific time and place.

If he had not widened his theological horizons at Wheaton College, if he had adhered strictly to his fundamentalist leanings, he would have decided that Ruth was not qualified to be his wife.

But he had changed. He was not encased in a straitjacket of fundamentalist theology any longer. He had learned that conversion could be a many-sided experience. It came to different people in different ways. Determination of those who, whether by "crisis conversion" or by growth, had qualified for salvation was not man's job, but God's.

One other fact might have upset a strict Baptist: Ruth had never been baptized by immersion. Billy tried to persuade her to do so, using his best Southern Baptist arguments.

However, her Presbyterian answers were equally well rooted in the Scriptures, and she refused to be persuaded.

To this day, Billy Graham has a standing offer of one hundred dollars to any Baptist who can persuade Ruth to agree to immersion.

Grady Wilson summed up the attitude of all those who know Ruth:

"No hundred dollars of Billy's is ever so likely to stay unspent."

They graduated from Wheaton in June 1943, and were married in Montreat in August. They spent their seven-day, seventy-dollar honeymoon at Blowing Rock, North Carolina.

# CHAPTER SIX

# Western Springs

Billy Graham's first pastorate after his marriage paid him forty-five dollars a week. The church was located at Western Springs, not far from Wheaton.

There was no parsonage at all. Church services were simply held in the basement of a building. On the Sunday morning Billy started there, thirty-five people showed up. It was the total congregation.

He stayed at the First Baptist Church of Western Springs for sixteen months. During that time he increased the attendance to something over several hundred. Not only that, his zeal and enthusiasm were so real that he began to stir true feelings for religion in his flock.

By the time he left, he had started a building fund which was growing by leaps and bounds. As a result, the current minister of the church has an assistant. He also has a parsonage in which to live, and what he makes more or less approximates a living wage in the religious field.

Billy's theological program at Western Springs was three-pronged: Bible reading, prayer and evangelism. Every Sunday morning he preached the Gospel, and every Sunday evening he ran what would be called a revival meeting. At every appearance he ended his sermon with a call for "decisions for Christ." Almost always several people came forward.

His evangelism took in a wider range than that envisioned by most preachers. He included the evangelization of not only Western Springs but the entire world

in general. The effects of Billy Graham's boundless optimism are still felt in Western Springs. The tiny First
Baptist Church there now supports twenty missionaries
in all parts of the world.

It was during those early days of struggle at Western
Springs, while he was settling down not only into his
pastorate but also into married life, that another important person came into Billy's life.

Torrey Johnson was a Wheaton College graduate.
Older than Billy, he was a man of unbounded imagina-
tion, enthusiasm and energy. Upon leaving Wheaton he
had moved to Chicago and formed his own church, the
Midwest Bible Church of Cicero, Illinois.

Under Torrey's inspired guidance the Midwest Bible
Church became a center of evangelistic fervor. Torrey
was a modern man of the times, not content with doing
things the way his forebears had always done them.

Early on he had seen the advantages of the newest
medium of communication—radio—and had developed
a late-Sunday-night radio program to take advantage of
the instant communication it developed among thousands
of people he would never see.

The program was one hundred percent evangelistic
in aim. In addition to his own church, Torrey led religious rallies for a newly formed group called Youth
for Christ, which was to become extremely important
in the rise of Billy Graham. He also served as professor
of Greek at Northern Baptist Seminary in Chicago.

Torrey had heard Billy preach once at Wheaton, and
marked him as a forthright and forceful evangelist. Upon
his arrival at Western Springs, Billy met Torrey several
times and the two men sat down together and discussed
their professions and their religious convictions.

At the time Billy was toying with the idea of going
on to theological school. He had spent four years at
Florida Bible Institute and three at Wheaton, but he
felt that there was a great deal he could still learn about
religion.

Torrey persuaded him not to. A practical man who
had no patience with the rigors and disciplines of theol-

ogy, he warned Billy that too much study might tend
to inhibit a natural evangelist. He advised Billy simply
to preach and preach and preach. According to Torrey,
action was the only theological school that Billy needed
to attend.

Early in 1944 Torrey Johnson telephoned Billy Graham from his office in Chicago:

"I'm getting heavily involved in my own church
work, and the Youth for Christ rallies. I've just got too
much to do and I can't give my best to my Sunday evening radio program."

Billy sympathized with him, and wondered why Torrey had called.

Torrey didn't leave him in doubt long:

"I want you and your church to take it over."

Billy was surprised and gratified that Torrey should
call him. He was only one year out of college, and a
neophyte in many ways. Billy knew it was the chance
of a lifetime—something God must have had a hand in.

"Our little church on the air," Billy said later, "fifty
thousand watts strong, spreading the Gospel!"

Further conversation pinpointed one major hitch in
the plan. Billy's church membership numbered eighty-
five at that time. His weekly church budget was one
hundred and twenty-five dollars, and some weeks he
could barely meet that.

"How much does the radio time cost?" Billy asked
in a practical manner.

When Torrey told him it was a hundred and fifty
dollars a week, Billy's spirits sagged. But only for a
time.

He acted the same way evangelists have acted from
the time of Jesus Christ, and called his congregation together to consider the matter. While they prayed for
guidance, they opened up their pocketbooks. Weekly
pledges of eighty-five dollars were forthcoming.

That was only a little more than half enough.

No matter how hard the members of his congregation squeezed, they could not seem to produce any
more money.

"Such an opportunity may never come our way again," Billy said. "Let's sign up and trust God for the rest."

His congregation agreed.

Thus, on a wing and a prayer, began *Songs in the Night,* an informal, family-circle type of Gospel singing with Billy Graham. It was broadcast over Chicago radio station WENR on Sunday evenings from 10:30 to 11:15.

Along with the singing, Billy read selections from the Bible and conducted prayers. In between the music and prayer he mixed in three- to five-minute chats on religion, based on stories from the Bible and conceived in line with Billy's evangelistic leanings.

The way Billy Graham put together the program appealed immediately to people in the Chicago area who tuned in. Contributions began to come in from the very first broadcast, literally out of thin air. In a very short while the program was being paid for entirely by contributions from listeners.

When the success of his radio program was solidly rooted, his congregation decided to add a "personality" to the show. On Chicago's radio station WMBI at the time there was an announcer and singer who was known to the entire area. Billy hired George Beverly Shea as a paid soloist for the singing sections of the program. To this day, George Beverly Shea is "America's beloved Gospel singer," and one of the top-echelon members of the Billy Graham team.

Each radio program wound up with Billy's call for "decisions for Christ." Although of course these "decisions" were not immediately apparent to Billy, because he was communicating with people for miles around whom he could not see, it soon became evident that there were many hundreds of them. The converts wrote in to tell him so.

The decisions increased at a rapid rate. Billy Graham became known far beyond the borders of the small town where he preached. Dozens of invitations poured in to him at the tiny church in Western Springs, asking him to conduct revival services, to preach and to speak at banquets.

To this day *Songs in the Night* is still being broadcast. It still uses the same program format that Billy Graham originated. It still comes from the same church, "the friendly church in the pleasant community of Western Springs, Illinois," as the radio announcement has it.

At the time *Songs in the Night* started, Billy Graham had been accepted by the United States Army as a chaplain and was waiting for assignment. In the cold winter days in Chicago, he caught the mumps and was sick for several months. His sickness led to his discharge from the Army chaplaincy.

His recuperation from the disease took a long time. An anonymous donor in his congregation sent him a gift of money, specifying only that it be spent "in the sunshine."

Billy took Ruth to Florida, where they settled into a hotel. Hardly had they begun to enjoy their stay there when the telephone rang.

It was Torrey Johnson, whom Billy hadn't seen for many months. He was staying at the same hotel and had seen Billy and Ruth check in. It was very strange, he said, but he had been thinking of Billy and wanted to talk to him about something that had come up.

Billy Graham later wrote: "It was not by chance that we met. The Lord was in it."

The two men renewed their acquaintance, which had begun at Wheaton, been renewed at Western Springs, and reinforced by Torrey's decision on *Songs in the Night*.

They talked together, took walks and prayed together. Torrey told Billy that he had a great dream of an international evangelistic movement among young people. But it was a big job and he was bogged down in details and couldn't get it started right.

He had joined the movement called Youth for Christ and become its recognized national leader. The organization of young Protestants was started in 1943 by the Reverend Roger Malsbary, pastor of the Christian and

Missionary Alliance Church in Indianapolis. Other fundamentalist pastors had met with Malsbary and had held the first Youth for Christ Conference during the Winona Lake Bible Conference in July 1944.

From the beginning, the group had grown phenomenally among servicemen throughout the United States and overseas. Youth for Christ specialized in mass evangelism, with Saturday-night Youth for Christ rallies held wherever there were sponsors.

The group was given wide publicity by publisher William Randolph Hearst, and by the end of 1944 there were four hundred cities conducting Youth for Christ rallies. Hearst believed that such groups did a lot of good in combating the upsurge of juvenile delinquency caused by wartime dislocation of family life in America.

Hearst had become interested in Youth for Christ when it began breaking records for attendance in Los Angeles, Hearst's home base. He promoted it with several editorials in his national chain of newspapers—not for religious reasons, but because he felt it provided moral standards for youth in a time of upheaval. And he ran articles through International News Service, his own news syndicate, which reached the heart of the nation through medium- and small-size cities and towns.

Torrey Johnson got the sincere backing of Christian War Veterans of America and other leading evangelist businessmen who believed that "Christ is the answer to juvenile delinquency."

In July 1945, Youth for Christ was reorganized into Youth for Christ International, with Torrey Johnson as president. The National Association of Evangelists gave the group its blessing, seeing it as an ally in winning young people away from the youth groups of the older church denominations.

The rallies were organized along tried-and-true evangelist lines, using the flamboyant techniques of old-fashioned revivalism, modernized to fit the times. They were held in large auditoriums, or in enormous stadiums, and the cities were plastered with posters to announce them ahead of time. Jazzy musical groups were worked into the programs, and other sensational aspects were added to keep the soldiers coming: ventriloquists, magicians, quartets singing harmony.

Pastors of old-fashioned churches downgraded Youth for Christ as "divisive, emotional, and spiritually shallow."

Youth for Christ had seven parts to its platform, and the first said: "We believe the Bible to be the inspired, the infallible authoritative Word of God." Because of this fundamentalist tenet and others, *Christian Century,* reflecting the "liberal" Protestant attitude, called the group "a streamlined expression of a traditionally conservative type of revivalism" which was "little concerned with the social or ethical bearing of the Christian faith."

Others in opposition to the group claimed it was "fascistic, antisemitic, and anti-Negro."

Because of the opposition by the more traditional liberalized Protestant church, Torrey Johnson had been told by the experts when he began running his rallies that he would never be able to get the kids to turn out on Saturday night. As usual, the know-it-alls were wrong. He began packing them into large halls, and one night he was able to fill Chicago's enormous Soldier Field.

Torrey was particularly excited now, he told Billy and Ruth Graham, because the time for the "big push" had come. He was trying to expand the program to include the entire United States and military and naval bases all over the world.

On the day Billy and Ruth were packed up to leave for Chicago, Torrey came in to see them.

He had a surprise for Billy. "I want you to be part of the worldwide push for Youth for Christ, Billy," he said. "I want you to become YFC's first field representative."

Billy was flabbergasted. "But what'll I do about my pastorate?"

"It's your decision," said Torrey. "But you'll get seventy-five dollars a week plus expenses working for

Youth for Christ. I've got two supporters in Chicago who have just pledged it."

Billy was in a turmoil. "Let me think it over," he pleaded with Torrey.

Torrey agreed.

Billy and Ruth talked it over.

"You'll have to give up the pastorate," Ruth said.

"That's right," Billy said. "And take up what the Lord's really called me to do—evangelism."

Ruth was practical. "There's only one thing left to settle," she said.

Billy nodded.

"Me. What am *I* going to do? It's certainly not practical to start hiking all over the country with you."

"Not for a while, anyway," Billy agreed.

They decided that she would move to Montreat. And so, after they returned to Chicago, Ruth moved in temporarily with her parents in North Carolina. Moving was less than a chore—the Grahams didn't own a piece of furniture.

Billy joined Torrey, and the two of them officially opened a bare two-room office in the midst of Chicago's bustling Loop one day in 1945.

There they got down on their knees in the center of the room and asked God's blessing on their plans and dreams for reaching young people around the world for Christ.

The first Youth for Christ rally that Billy Graham held was in Orchestra Hall in Chicago. Billy was slated to deliver a twenty-minute sermon. The audience was around three thousand.

The prospect of talking to that many people at one time scared Billy. He remembered the old fright and embarrassment he had felt back in Tampa when he had run out to the swamp to preach to the birds and the cypress stumps.

"It was the worst case of stage fright in my life," Billy recalled. "I shook in my boots. But as my nerves relaxed, I felt I was merely a mouthpiece and soon became unaware of the audience."

After his sermon he gave the call, and was pleased to see that forty young men came forward and made their decisions for Christ.

In the next twelve months, Billy Graham flew almost two hundred thousand miles around the country, organizing Youth for Christ rallies in cities that did not have them and conducting rally services for groups in existence.

He spoke in forty-seven states to Youth for Christ rallies, each one drawing up to twenty thousand people. During that year at least seven thousand young people made the decision for Christ.

One night in Asheville, North Carolina, the regular song leader failed to appear at the rally. A local aide in charge of the rally mentioned to Billy that there was a young man in the audience who had some experience as a song leader.

Billy hesitated. Leading the singing was much too important to be left to an amateur.

Finally he approached the tyro singer and reluctantly asked him if he would take over.

The singer, as reluctant as Billy, didn't think he could do a good enough job.

There was nothing for it but to give the young man a chance. Billy told him to go ahead.

After one or two songs, Billy turned to the chairman who had suggested the youth. "He's great. What did you say his name was?"

"Cliff Barrows."

That night Cliff Barrows joined Billy Graham, and he has been with him ever since. In the history of evangelism, many of the most effective preachers have made success possible by teaming up with a good song leader. For example, John Wesley had his brother Charles; Moody had Ira Sankey; and Billy Sunday had Wesley Rhodeheaver.

Cliff Barrows, Stanley High wrote, is probably closer to Billy Graham than any other member of the team. His counsel is continually sought on many matters besides music.

"He comes near to being the indispensable man," Billy Graham once noted.

For three years Billy Graham continued as field representative for Youth for Christ. During that time he logged 750,000 miles, including four trips to Europe.

In spite of the success of the group, there was still a great deal of opposition.

*Christian Century* printed a diatribe against Youth for Christ, but at the end admitted:

> Yet the fact that it has gone so far as it has is proof that something close to spiritual famine exists among large sections of our population, including the rising generation, who are more hungry for faith than their elders.
>
> The churches are not feeding these starving people and they cannot be indifferent to the challenge which this attempt to use the new channels of communication for preaching the Gospel offers them. They should do likewise, and better.

On a trip to England in 1946, Billy found that the Birmingham City Council had withdrawn permission for him to use the city auditorium for his rallies. The action came as the result of opposition to the meeting from local ministers.

Billy went to the clergymen, calling on them one by one, and discussed, coolly, the reasons he was anxious to reach the youths in Birmingham. One by one he won them over, and the City Council eventually rescinded its action at the request of a group of clergymen.

Most of his opposition came from the churches, chiefly among conservative ministers. Some of them thought that the theology of evangelists was not of "solid meat" but of "milky abstractions." Others protested that the techniques smacked of "business and commercial radio."

The churches generally considered all evangelists "Christian gypsies." They didn't like to think that simple Gospel messages could rouse people in a science-

minded, socially sophisticated world—particularly
young people. One of the Birmingham ministers later
wrote about the visiting Youth for Christ rallies:

> I wasn't interested. We had plenty of soul-winners
> right here in Birmingham, without taking on any of
> America's surplus saints.
> But Billy called on me. He wasn't bitter, just won-
> dering. I ended up wanting to hug the twenty-seven-
> year-old boy. I had failed. I called my church officers
> and we disrupted all our plans for the nine days of
> his visit.
> Before it was over, Birmingham had seen a touch
> of God's blessing. This fine, lithe, burning torch of
> a man made me love him and his Lord.

In 1948 Youth for Christ became aggressively evangelistic, and Billy Graham was the spearhead for city-
wide revival services designed to win more persons over
to the "spiritual ecumenicalism" of born-again believers.

In the three years of his field service Billy Graham
managed to meet most of the leaders in the fundamentalism camp and was associated with most of the revivalists in the National Association of Evangelists, whose
magazine featured his activities regularly.

Also, Billy gained valuable experience in organizing
large-scale evangelical rallies in theaters, auditoriums
and football stadiums. As a field representative he did
not go alone but as a member of a team of young evangelists who shared his background and outlook.

The slogan of Youth for Christ was: "Geared to the
times, but anchored to the Rock." The "Rock" referred
to Biblical fundamentalism. The "timeliness" referred
to evangelical techniques.

"We used every modern means to catch the ear of
unconverted young people and then punched them
straight between the eyes with the Gospel," Billy Graham reported later.

Whatever the reason, it was working very well, and
Billy was coming along at what seemed to him an almost frightening pace.

# CHAPTER SEVEN

# President

Billy Graham's quite obvious success with his evangelistic preaching was noticed not only by the public but, as might be expected, by other members of the clergy as well.

One of those most interested in the effectiveness of any young, up-and-coming preacher was Dr. William Bell Riley. Once as he sat on the platform of a Youth for Christ rally listening to an address by Billy, he commented: "That young man never misses the bull's-eye."

Riley was an old-time evangelist who had spent many years at the pulpit preaching a fiery type of sermon to his audiences. For all his old-fashioned sulfur-and-brimstone delivery, he was an astute businessman blessed with common sense and more than his share of intelligence.

He was pastor of the First Baptist Church of Minneapolis in 1902. In that year he founded an interdenominational school called the Northwestern Bible Training Institute. It was housed in a building adjacent to his church.

He added a theological seminary to the Institute in 1935, and a college of liberal arts in 1944. By that time the school and all its colleges had changed its name to Northwestern Schools.

Riley was an original thinker who loved to read books of all kinds. In fact, he wrote a number himself. Like most authors, he was a man of strong convictions, frequently taking controversial positions on hotly argued issues.

Nevertheless, he was a man who could make even his enemies love him. He had a shrewd native understanding of psychology, and could make people do what he wanted them to. He was also used to getting his own way.

As in many of the Bible schools in the South, teaching and training at Northwestern Schools was centered in the Bible and dedicated to the evangelist way.

As Dr. Riley grew older he began to worry about who was going to succeed him as head of the institution he had created. Finally he settled on the one man he thought would be best for the job.

Not surprisingly, that man was Billy Graham.

In 1946 he called Billy to Minneapolis and began to talk to him as if he were going to be the next president of Northwestern Schools.

He told Billy it could be "one of the greatest Christian colleges of the nation" under his tutelage. "Great buildings with hundreds of students—a school that stands firmly and positively for the essentials of the faith. A place whose ministry reaches the ends of the earth."

Billy shook his head. He told Riley that he did not have the proper training to run a university. He suggested that Torrey Johnson might be the man for the job. Billy said that if Torrey would take the job, he would be glad to work as Torrey's assistant.

When Riley asked him, Johnson refused.

Riley came back to Billy. Again Billy declined the offer.

The old evangelist was not the kind of man who would take "no" for a final answer, especially when he had his own mind set on "yes."

He wrote a letter to Billy, who was on the road for Youth for Christ, and posted it in the next mail with an alternative. Not only did he have a compromise offer, but he had Biblical quotations to bolster it, pointing out that it wasn't really only his plan, but God's plan as well.

The compromise offer was that Billy Graham would

serve in his presidential duties at Northwestern Schools
for four days a week and continue working for Youth
for Christ for three days a week.

To Dr. Riley's offer, Billy responded:

> I have sought to discern the will of God. If God
> has blessed me with a particular field it has been
> that of an evangelist.
>
> I told the Lord two years ago that I did not care
> to be a great preacher, but that I did want to be a
> great soul-winner.
>
> How to reconcile work at Northwestern with the
> tremendous evangelistic opportunities open to me is
> difficult.
>
> May I have until July 21?

Dr. Riley granted the extension.

In July Billy wrote again:

"I have been waiting for heaven's signal. I have not
received it."

In August 1947 the old man, now eighty-six, pleaded
with Billy to come visit him at his home in Golden
Valley.

The bedridden Riley, obviously dying, greeted Billy,
not with pleas but with an immediate challenge that
made Billy wonder where he had gotten the strength.

"Billy, you are the man to succeed me; I've known
it for a long time. You will be disobeying God if you
don't!"

Fumbling for his Bible, Riley opened it to the pas-
sage in which Elijah, as he goes up to heaven, drops
the mantle of his office upon Elisha. "I'm leaving this
school to you as Elijah gave his mantle to Elisha. I
leave you this school!"

To the evangelistic fraternity, a very closely knit one,
Riley was something of a father figure. Billy was flat-
tered and at the same time worried. He was concerned
that he was not the proper choice; he felt still that the
force of his talent was in another direction.

He procrastinated for some time, discussing with

Ruth the important decision that he must make. He felt that with him evangelism came first. However, as president of an independent theological college he would be able to travel. The problem was that inevitably the two jobs would conflict with each other.

He was worried too that his background was not right for the job. And he did not really think that he wanted to be associated with the Midwest fundamentalism implicit in the theological leanings of the school. Fundamentalism had negative connotations so far as Billy was concerned.

Actually, in 1947 "fundamentalism" had different meanings for different people.

Liberal Protestants who considered themselves modern used the word to put down any man who clung to Biblical literality in preference to scientific facts.

To Billy Graham it was a synonym for "evangelism" —proclaiming a Biblical gospel in the Reformation heritage of Luther and Calvin, Wesley and Whitefield.

To Riley it meant anyone who would debate for the "verities of God's Word."

To some of the members of Riley's board of directors it meant a narrow and literal interpretation of the faith, hemmed in by the actual words and not the spirit of the Bible.

Billy had by now decided that his aim in life was to bring as many people into the Christian faith as he could. Such an extensive and far-reaching ambition might be thwarted by connection with Northwestern Schools, which was already known by some for its blasts against modernism.

In September 1947 Billy agreed finally that if Riley should die within the next ten months he would become interim president of Northwestern Schools, so long as his commitments to Youth for Christ International and other evangelistic projects could be fulfilled.

In an earlier published version of this pact, incidentally, biographer Stanley High wrote that Dr. Riley quoted not the story of Elijah but the story of Samuel to persuade Billy to accept the presidency.

It was Samuel's duty to choose a king from among the sons of Jesse. The choice was a difficult one. When Samuel chose the youngest in the family—David—Jehovah said:

"Arise, anoint him; for this is he."

Then, Dr. Riley continued, "Beloved, as Samuel appointed David King of Israel, so I appoint you head of these schools. I'll meet you at the judgment seat of Christ with them."

Quite possibly the dying old man used both arguments.

In November 1947, Billy Graham, Cliff Barrows, George Beverly Shea and Grady Wilson, who was then a pastor in South Carolina but quit to join Billy, started a three-week evangelical campaign in the South. It was at Hattiesburg, Mississippi, at a Youth for Christ rally, that George Wilson, the business manager of Northwestern Schools, telephoned Billy and told him that Riley had died.

Billy kept his word. He became interim president of the college. Characteristically, he plunged into the new venture with total enthusiasm and dedication. His first move was to take stock of the administrative setup and make a few changes.

He kept George Wilson as business manager. George, incidentally, was no relation to Grady and T. W. Wilson, Billy's boyhood friends. Grady was working with Billy at the time, and T. W. was pastor of a church in the South.

Billy telephoned T. W. to suggest that he join Northwestern Schools as a vice-president of the organization. T. W. turned his old friend down.

Eight nights in a row Billy telephoned T. W., until their friendship was almost compromised. Billy was as persistent with his friend as Dr. Riley had been with Billy. Eventually T. W. agreed to take the job, but it was several months later.

In 1948 the combined student body of the schools numbered 739 students, with about 200 enrolled in night courses. The physical college plant had been improved, and one new building was ready for occupancy. But the treasury was almost empty.

Quickly Billy went to work. The new motto for Northwestern Schools became "Knowledge on Fire," typical of Billy's zest and bounce.

Immediately he began to reconstruct the curricula of the various schools in order to bring accreditation. He wanted the college to be structured like Wheaton College.

However, he found that it was not quite so easy to restructure an entire college curriculum. Even though his objectives were completely right, it was difficult to move swiftly in academia. But he had a sense of movement and zeal that did get things moving, even though not as fast as he would have liked.

What made his task so difficult as to be almost impossible, of course, was the fact that he refused to give up his evangelical efforts and his work for Youth for Christ to concentrate on Northwestern Schools.

John Pollock analyzed the problem:

He would sweep into Minneapolis from an evangelistic tour or campaign to stay a few days at a nearby hotel or rooming house. He would burst into the small presidential office in the new building on Willow Street overlooking Loring Park with its innumerable squirrels, and the hours would be packed with interviews, each nearly always including prayer.

He exuded optimism, made the place hum. "Give him five minutes and he'll think up enough projects to keep many staffs busy for months," exclaimed the devoted secretary he had inherited with the position, Luverne Gustavson.

Then would come a board meeting to discuss some measure, which really required research and careful scrutiny by faculty committees, but which he wished to see adopted in time for him to catch a plane. The discussion unfinished, he would look at his watch and turn to loyal T. W. Wilson.

"T, you better do the rest. Goodbye," and in a

few minutes his clothes would be stuffed once again higgledy-piggledy into a suitcase.

According to most of the people who saw how it worked, it was amazing that he did as well as he did. He had allowed himself to be put in an utterly impossible situation.

The fact was that during his years at Northwestern Schools the enrollment rose sharply, new buildings were occupied, a two-wave radio station was opened and the college magazine, *Northwestern Pilot,* achieved a circulation of thirty-five thousand, very good for a college publication.

However, Billy learned the hard way that a college could not be run by remote control.

"I hope you will understand and be very patient," he wrote in 1948 to Luverne. "When I neglect my correspondence from time to time in these campaigns, it is because I am so busy I hardly know what to do. I am speaking four or five times a day and trying to prepare all these messages and keep my body fit and my soul prepared before the Lord, and it is awfully hard to get to any of this other work, but I am trying to fill in between the cracks."

The stint at Northwestern Schools was not lost time for Billy, however. He learned a great deal about the "educator category" of the ministry mentioned by St. Paul in the Bible. He had already learned at the small church in Western Springs about the "pastor category."

Billy knew now that he had the natural "gift" for neither. What was left to him at this point was evangelism. He knew he would have to make his way in that field or nowhere.

And his years at Northwestern Schools gave him invaluable training in finance, promotion and administration. They helped teach him the delegation of responsibility, the importance of tapping the right sources of advice, and the molding of a team.

He brought in new blood, and several men and

women who were later to work together with him on a
wider scope met him through Northwestern.

There had been divisions in the administration before
Billy Graham arrived, as there so often are in institutions of higher education. Petty jealousies constantly
thwarted Billy's plans. Dissent at board meetings frus-
trated him.

For the first time, he tasted complete failure in a
venture. He had been opposed often, but in establishing
a rally or launching a campaign he knew how to overcome the difficulties and woo the opposition.

At Northwestern there was a constant gap between
purpose and achievement. The disapproval of high and
powerful figures could not be ignored, and the problem
of their opposition would not simply go away.

Yet the difficulties he experienced at Northwestern
put steel into Billy Graham's spirit, steel that was there
when he needed it later in moments of adversity.

For three and a half years the strife continued, with
Billy leading what amounted to a schizophrenic, two-
sided life. Under him, the school prospered and grew.
So did Billy's evangelistic career.

But, as often happened to religious figures at moments of great activity, doubts began to assail him. He
began to fear that perhaps he was taking the Bible too
literally. Perhaps he was being bound in by precepts
he had accepted on faith.

Finally, in June 1951, he decided he had to resign.
In his resignation letter he said:

"I have been trying to do the work of two men. It
isn't working. I must choose one or the other. The leading of the Lord seems clear and I must follow it."

Actually, in 1949 he had begun to feel doubts about
his calling generally. There had been trouble in filling
halls in some cities as his team moved from place to
place. It seemed that his sermons were stale and flat,
and his calls went unanswered.

At this low point in his career he and his colleagues
decided to make one last-ditch try for one of the big
cities. It was a boom-or-bust situation. They chose

Los Angeles, a sprawling metropolis that was growing like wildfire.

Before the rigors of the three-week crusade, Billy decided to go to a camp in the mountains to meditate just before the opening.

A group of his theological friends were there. He was invited to speak. He gave them a very typical, staunchly fundamentalist sermon, the kind he had been delivering for the past ten years.

Later that night he accidentally overheard an old and dear friend—an aged preacher—talking about him to others.

"Poor Billy," the old man was saying. "He's still preaching a literal Bible. It's not going to work. He's got those old-fashioned ideas of theology that are not going to be listened to in our generation."

Billy was terribly hurt.

"I slipped away to my cottage alone," he related later. "I knelt down by the bed and wept. I opened my Bible and prayed. I said, 'O God, am I wrong? Is this Your true word? Or is it what some people claim—just man-written history, myth, and poetry?'

"And then the greatest peace, the greatest assurance, came over me. I said, 'O God, I can't understand all that's in this book. But I am going to accept this book by faith, as Your revelation to man, Your word, Your message to the human race.'

"My mind was completely made up. I have never known a moment's doubt since then. This decision gave a power and authority to my preaching that has never left me. The gospel in my hands became a hammer and a flame."

# CHAPTER EIGHT

# City of the Angels

Even though Los Angeles dates back to the middle part of the nineteenth century, when it was a tiny pueblo, or mission stop, in the mission system established by the Franciscan Fathers in the time of the Spanish conquistadors, it is typically and completely a twentieth-century city.

Its phenomenal growth started at the turn of the century. It owed its fantastic prosperity and size to the automobile, a twentieth-century development. It owed its population growth not to a high birthrate but to immigrants from all parts of the country.

Many of these migrants came from the Midwest. Almost as many came from the South. Others came from New England. The religious background of these immigrants was quite overwhelmingly Protestant. These Protestants had come usually from small towns and had worshipped in small churches of a generally conservative type.

In Los Angeles, which grew outward and not upward, as most other cities before it had grown, there was only one massive community spreading out rapidly from an epicenter, without smaller local centers as satellites. It was in effect an enormous suburb.

Churches sprang up here and there, but for most of the displaced Protestants used to small-town church meetings, the churches that emerged were not familiar and seemed remote and unfriendly. Because Protestants congregated voluntarily and not by compulsion, as many other religions did, these people tended to break off from church attendance and membership. Almost two generations of Angelenos had grown up as Protestants who did not go to any specific Protestant church or join any specific sect. Even the blacks—overwhelmingly Protestant—did not have enough churches to go to, and had generally lost touch with their religious leaders.

With the ending of World War II in the autumn of 1945, and the subsequent return of millions of GIs who had a little money in their pockets and a desire now to settle where they *wanted* to live, the influx of Americans into the Los Angeles area was almost frightening in its dimensions.

These incoming postwar Protestants constituted another mass of nondenominational Americans who were Protestant but had no specific place to worship. With the pressures of war behind them, they went busily to work at new jobs, married and began raising families.

Millions of them had lost their lifeline to religion.

That was the situation in Los Angeles four years after the end of World War II.

In early September 1949, Billy Graham and his evangelist team began a three-week stand in Los Angeles. With his three associates—Grady Wilson, associate evangelist; Cliff Barrows, director of music; and George Beverly Shea, soloist and trombonist—they organized the most far-reaching pre-revival campaign they had ever tackled.

Organized prayer support was set up weeks in advance under the auspices of an organization called Christ for Greater Los Angeles, which included Christian Endeavor, Youth for Christ and the Gideons, among other groups. At least a thousand prayer groups were formed in and around Los Angeles weeks before the revival began.

For several weeks the groups met regularly to pray for the success of the campaign. There were also "prayer chains" that continued all during the revival itself.

These volunteers were recruited by Grady Wilson

at the meetings. They divided the day and night into half-hour periods so that for twenty-four hours a day, around the clock, prayers continued for the Billy Graham revival.

From the first day, the Los Angeles campaign was a success. The revival tent, set up on a huge vacant lot at Washington Boulevard and Hill Street in the shadow of Los Angeles' few mid-city skyscrapers, filled at each session. The "Canvas Cathedral" held a little over six thousand.

Crowds swelled every night. In fact, the throngs began growing in the third week. Several of the committee were ready to call it quits at the scheduled time, satisfied with the results obtained even if most of the millions who lived in the huge Los Angeles area were not aware of Billy Graham at all.

Others in the team argued for an extension. The decision finally went to Billy. A check of the attendance records showed that the turnout had been good, and that it had begun to rise in the middle of the third and final week. Would it continue to rise? No one knew. Billy Graham had never extended a campaign before. Was it worth it, or would it all fizzle out?

Billy decided to go to the Gospel for his answer. In the Book of Judges young Gideon had been called upon by the Lord to deliver Israel from bondage. Gideon did not know if the call was a true one from God or a temptation of the devil.

> And Gideon said unto God, If thou wilt save Israel by mine hand, as thou hast said,
> Behold, I will put a fleece of wool in the floor; and if the dew be on the fleece only, and it be dry upon all the earth besides, then shall I know thou wilt save Israel by mine hand, as thou hast said.
> And it was so: for he rose up early on the morrow, and thrust the fleece together, and wringed the dew out of the fleece, a bowl full of water. (Judges 6:36–38)

Billy Graham told God he was going to "put out the fleece" and watch for a sign. The sign came in the middle of the night on one of the last days of the third week. It came in the form of a telephone call.

At that time, a colorful ex-cowpoke from Texas named Stuart Hamblen was one of the most successful country-western singers on the West Coast. He was the star of his own radio program over KFWB, the Warner Brothers radio outlet in Los Angeles.

Born in Texas, Hamblen had been brought up in a strict Methodist family; his father was a minister of the Gospel. Young Hamblen grew up straight and tall in physical aspect, but didn't take to education or religion.

By the time he was a teen-ager, he had dropped out of school and was doing just about what he wanted to do. "I was heading straight for hell," he said later, "and I figured I might just as well enjoy the ride."

His father took a long, jaundiced look at him one day, and decided he needed some guidance. He sent him to Reed Double Circle ranch in the Texas Panhandle for shaping up.

Hamblen learned a lot about cattle, about horses and about singing on the ranch. He had sung before, in church, but on the ranch he learned to sing at night to keep the cows gentled. It was an old cowboy skill; every night the sweet sound of old-fashioned tunes floated over the range.

He found out he liked to sing, and learned all the great songs known to country-western singers. It was a type of music not generally accepted by city folks or "civilized" Americans.

After he left the ranch he drifted about Texas, singing at barbecues, festivals and sometimes nightclubs, doing odd jobs when he could get them. He won a contest once, singing "The Johnstown Flood."

It was no way to make a living, and Hamblen bummed his way out to the West Coast. He had heard there was money to be made on the radio there.

When he hit Los Angeles, he walked out to Hollywood, and was standing on a street corner when a man came up to him and said:

"I like you, boy. Why don't you come up to my room for a drink?"

Hamblen knew a homosexual when he saw one, and immediately punched him in the nose. A crowd gathered, and the crowd began punching Hamblen. He ran, saving himself from further harm by jumping onto a bus.

That was enough of Los Angeles for him. He returned to Texas. There, on the eve of a job interview at a Ford plant, he was arrested in a poolroom after someone called the cops under the mistaken assumption that he intended to *rob* the Ford plant.

A bruiser of a cop slammed him against the wall and booked him. He was held on an "open charge," which meant he could be kept in the pokey forever if need be.

His father heard about his plight and came to town to spring him. Hamblen returned to Los Angeles. This time he got a chance to audition for a radio show that was playing at night—the *Midnight Jamboree.*

Don Wilson, who later came to fame as Jack Benny's radio announcer, was running the audition. He and a studio executive were in the control room when Hamblen started singing "The Johnstown Flood."

Wilson and the exec were sophisticates who had been around cities for a long time, and Hamblen's singing really broke them up. They couldn't laugh hard enough, and held their sides to keep from splitting.

Hamblen was annoyed and stopped in the middle of the number. "If you clowns don't like my singing, I can go somewhere else."

"No, no," Wilson said, gasping for breath. "We'll give you a shot at it. How'd you like to be on the *Midnight Jamboree?*"

Hamblen went on the show. He was an almost instant success. City types like Wilson didn't realize that a large percentage of Los Angeles at that time had immigrated from Iowa, Kansas, Oklahoma, Texas, Colorado and the heartland states of America. Country music was their thing.

From that slim beginning, Hamblen became a big, big star. Soon he had his own show, called the *Covered Wagon Jamboree.* Then he was the star of *Stuart Hamblen's Lucky Stars.* By the late 1940s he was making a thousand dollars a week.

He poured his radio money into the things he loved best: racing horses. His time at the Reed Double Circle ranch had taught him how to judge horseflesh. He bred racing horses, and knew how to pick winners. He was soon making money at the track as well as on the radio.

And he was spending it—on bets, on food, on friends and on hunting, for which he had an outdoorsman's passion. Money was a new thing for him. He dined well, and soon began to wine well. The money he earned attracted friends of all kinds—savory and unsavory— to his side.

One day he saw a pretty girl pass him on the street. He ran up to stop her. She looked even more beautiful when she told him to mind his own business.

"I'm going to marry you," he announced. "What's your name?"

Her name was Suzy, and she did marry him, but not until he had gotten rid of a fiancé by scaring him out of town.

Suzy loved her husband, but didn't like his drinking habits and didn't like many of his friends. She was a devout Christian, and belonged to an informal organization called the Hollywood Christian Group. Many actors and actresses belonged to it.

She tried to get Hamblen interested, but he couldn't be bothered. He kept remembering his father and those early confrontations with the church.

In September 1949 Suzy got her husband to attend one meeting of the group. Billy Graham had been invited to it to talk about opening up his tent campaign in Los Angeles.

Hamblen almost backed out at the last minute, but

Suzy exerted her will on him, and they arrived an hour early at the meeting place in Westwood, the home of Henrietta Mears. Oddly enough, Billy Graham was there an hour early, too.

The two opposites took to each other almost immediately. Hamblen liked the clean-cut Southern boy. "Hey," he told him. "You come on my radio show. I can fill that tent down there for you!"

Hamblen was as good as his word. When Billy appeared on the radio, the two of them chatted about religion and religious songs, and Hamblen wound up the show by urging all his listeners to go down to the Canvas Cathedral.

"I'll be there too," he added at the last minute.

And he was. He and Suzy were right down in the front row, like patrons of the arts. Hamblen showed up every night for the first week, figuring the publicity wasn't hurting him at all.

The second week Hamblen wasn't smiling quite so much. He didn't like the way Billy seemed to be baiting him.

"Someone in this tent is leading a double life," Billy said from the stage. "He's a hypocrite."

Hamblen knew the remarks were aimed at him. In the middle of the week he disappeared into the High Sierras on a hunting trip with some cronies.

He came back the third week. But Billy wouldn't let up. "There is a person in here tonight who is a phony" was the way Billy put it. Hamblen shook his fist at Billy and stalked out of the tent in the middle of the sermon.

Hamblen was beside himself with rage. That was what he got for helping this Bible-thumper! He went into one bar, then another, but the drinks tasted lousy. Besides, he didn't like the sound of the bands. They were hitting sour notes. He started home.

On the way home, he related later, Christ spoke to him. Hamblen ran in and woke up Suzy.

"Woman, get out of that bed!" he yelled at her.

"What on earth is the matter with you?"

"Let's pray!" Hamblen said.

She was puzzled and uneasy, but they got down on their knees and prayed.

"I couldn't make connections," Hamblen confessed.

They tried again. Hamblen was getting more and more rattled. Finally he got Billy Graham on the telephone. "I need you!" Hamblen said.

"Come on over to the apartment," Billy ordered him.

Hamblen and Suzy drove over to the place where the Graham entourage was staying. Billy let him in. Hamblen was beside himself with fear and anger.

"Billy," he yelled, "I want you to pray for me!"

"I'm not going to do it," Billy replied instantly.

Enraged at Billy's attitude, Hamblen almost knocked him flat.

"I'll tell you why, Stuart."

Billy told him the story from the Book of Matthew of the rich young ruler who wanted to achieve a selfish, easy faith. He pointed out to the cowboy singer that he would have to go all the way himself and give himself to Jesus Christ. Billy's prayers wouldn't do any good at all—for Hamblen.

Grady Wilson and his wife joined the Grahams and the Hamblens. It was about five in the morning when Hamblen finally broke down and said he was going to give up all that was "mean and wicked" in his heart.

He fell to his knees and began praying. The others joined in.

"I felt I was kneeling at the foot of my Jesus," Hamblen said later. "Lord," he prayed, "you're hearing a new voice this morning."

He was true to his word. The next day he told his radio audience what had happened to him: "I've quit smoking and I've quit drinking." He promised to sell his string of seven racehorses—except one. And he saved the big surprise for the punch line.

"Tonight at the end of Billy's invitation, I'm going to hit the sawdust trail."

Hundreds of strangers flocked to the big tent that night. Hamblen's broadcast was a breakthrough—for him *and* for Billy. The reaction was absolutely staggering. Crowds watched Hamblen as he made the "decision" at Billy's call.

Stuart Hamblen's conversion was Billy Graham's "fleece." With the concurrence of his staff, he extended the Los Angeles campaign one more week.

By the end of the week the excitement over the cowboy singer's conversion had subsided. Billy decided once more to fold the campaign. That night he came to the tent to find the place overrun with swarms of reporters and photographers. He had never seen so many newsmen. Photographers were climbing tent poles to get better shots of the crowd scene. Billy had to ask one cameraman to climb down so the audience could see him.

At the end of the sermon he was surrounded by press representatives. The next day the *Los Angeles Herald-Examiner* carried banner headlines.

Billy, bewildered, tried to find out what had happened to cause all the press excitement.

One of his aides finally got the answer: "You've been kissed by William Randolph Hearst."

It was true. The word had been passed along to his chain of newspapers by publisher Hearst: "Puff Graham." That meant, give Graham coverage and put his name in prominent headlines.

Hearst had always been partial to Youth for Christ. He remembered Billy Graham's work during the postwar years. Now, with the makings of a good story in Los Angeles, he instinctively reacted to the possibilities in Billy's charisma.

Puff Graham. The Hearst organization did just that.

The lengthy stories printed in the Hearst papers throughout the country were picked up by the Associated Press, and through AP reached newspapers in all corners of the country.

Billy was exhausted. He wanted to close the campaign. The rally had now gone on a lot longer than he had intended. He didn't want to push the people too hard—his own or the public.

And there was another reason. Weather reports said

a big storm was building in the Pacific Ocean. If it came in and brought rain with it, the Canvas Cathedral would be flooded out. There was good reason to fold up the tent and get out now.

He decided once again to put out the fleece to test his judgment. The storm was the key. And, to everybody's surprise, including the weather bureau, which had predicted rain, the storm fizzled at sea, blew itself out before it got to Los Angeles.

It was the sign Billy was waiting for.

He decided to keep the rally going another week.

# CHAPTER NINE

# On to Boston

Billy Graham was the talk of Los Angeles. Now all the reluctant converts, the people who had fallen from grace but who were too immersed in misery to know what to do, the hopeless, the helpless, the halt and the lame, knew that there was someone who might be able to help them.

Alcoholics, drug addicts, prostitutes, bums, thieves and many other dregs of humanity crowded around the big tent, too shy to enter, but begging for help from the counselors.

They got it.

Inside the tent, the more respectable elements of the community were listening with growing excitement to the handsome young man who was bringing them a message of strength and aid in a time of countrywide crisis.

An inner anxiety was gnawing away at the American psyche in 1949. Economically, the country was in excellent shape. People were working, were buying products superior to anything else manufactured in the world. They were free from war and its entanglements for the time being.

Yet the Cold War was casting a dark shadow of fear over them. Russia was testing its atomic bombs and threatening to overrun the rest of Europe, promising indeed to dominate and conquer it. In the East, China had gone Communist as a result of the pressures of the World War. The Chinese Communists were beginning to make noises of expansion. Little shooting wars flared up, then died down.

Materialism was comfortable, and life was easy in America, but the people knew that affluence and prosperity were not the be-all and end-all of life.

Man, as Jesus Christ had said, did not live by bread alone.

What these people found in Billy Graham's Canvas Cathedral on Washington Boulevard was not a man who knew all the answers to all the sticky problems of the world. Instead, they found a man who preached the truths of the Bible straight out of the Good Book.

And Billy Graham had changed, too. No longer was he worried about whether or not the Word of the Bible was true or false. He *knew* it was true. He simply read its word and gave people the messages from the Gospel.

Even local ministers who had not been completely ecstatic at the prospect of an evangelistic revival in Los Angeles were experiencing a change of heart. They now realized that the public's interest in Christianity had been spurred beyond their wildest dreams.

One minister said, "This city, with its thousand ministers preaching every Sunday, was going lazily along with the man in the street unimpressed. Then came Billy Graham. In eight weeks, he had more people talking about the claims of Christ than had all the city's pulpiteers in a year's time.

"When the Crusade closed, we faced a community that was at least willing to talk about the claims of Christ. My church got a dozen members, but it got more than members. It got new inspiration, zeal and a spiritual uplift that can never be described."

There was more to come.

*Time* and *Newsweek* both picked up the story and highlighted the country's "new evangelist."

Another of Billy Graham's converts of national reputation was the son of poor Italian Roman Catholic immigrants. His name was Louis Zamperini. He had distinguished himself in the Berlin Olympics of 1936 by being the youngest long-distance runner to compete.

Incensed that the Reichstag's swastika was flying above the American flag, Zamperini won international press coverage by climbing up and pulling it off the staff.

Later on, during World War II, he was almost lost at sea when his ship went down in the Pacific. Half dead, he floated on a bobbing raft for forty-seven days until he was found by the Japanese. He spent the balance of the war in a prison camp, undergoing rigorous tortures at the hands of his captors.

He never fully recovered from the physical and psychological atrocities. Upon his return to California he was a broken man, unable to sleep without suffering incredibly hideous nightmares.

In addition, he had been listed as dead. His dramatic return to life resulted in a great deal of publicity. He got a huge insurance payment from the War Department, but managed to run through it in record time.

Unable to locate a job, he could not support himself or his wife, Cynthia, who was desperate for help for her husband. She attended the Canvas Cathedral to listen to Billy Graham in a last-ditch attempt to find some way out of her dilemma. She answered Billy's call. When she returned home, elated and almost dazed with hope, she told her husband:

"For the first time in my life I have peace in my heart."

Zamperini was skeptical of her new-found faith. When she asked him to go with her next time to see Billy Graham, he told her he didn't want to.

But when the next day came, and he had nothing else to do anyway, he went with her.

Billy Graham stirred something deep in the psyche of the athlete and war hero. Zamperini saw that Billy Graham was everything that was fine in the one world he understood: athletics. Billy was built like an athlete; he carried himself like one. To Zamperini, Billy was more like an athlete than a man of God.

That didn't mean that Zamperini was buying Billy's religious ideas, though. In no way!

Disgusted at what seemed to him a "holier-than-thou" attitude in Billy's preachings, the long-distance runner stomped out of the tent in the middle of the sermon.

What Billy said had really cut too close to the bone, Zamperini admitted later. He only wanted to get far away from Billy Graham and everything he stood for.

Yet two nights later he was back with his wife.

When the call came, he yielded and made the decision for Christ.

"From now on," he said, "I am going to be an honest-to-God Christian."

Zamperini's conversion made more headlines.

Billy Graham was totally exhausted now. The campaign was heading into its eighth week—five weeks beyond its original schedule.

"The weaker I get physically, the stronger I get spiritually," he remarked.

On Sunday, November 20, the Graham team closed out the Los Angeles campaign. The big tent had been enlarged to seat nine thousand—three thousand seats more than when the campaign began. No one could really estimate the total audience. Newsmen claimed that it was almost certainly the largest religious gathering since Billy Sunday's 1917 New York campaign.

"We had gone to Los Angeles unheralded," Billy Graham said. "When we left we knew that the Spirit of God had moved on that California city as never before. We believed also that there He gave proof that He would bless and use our ministry 'exceeding abundantly, above all that we ask or think.'"

*Time* quoted him: "We are standing on the verge of a great national revival, an old-fashioned, heaven-sent Holy Ghost revival that will sweep the nation. In the words of Joel: 'Put in the sickle while the harvest is ripe.'"

Calling him a "blond, trumpet-lunged" preacher in typical *Time* style, the newsmagazine described how he used a lapel mike to amplify his "deep cavernous voice," and how he paced about the platform, rising on his toes, clenching his fists and stabbing his finger at the sky.

"Mr. Graham," the magazine reported, "is as modern as the flashy handpainted tie he wears and as colorful as his advertising."

The story also quoted him as saying:

"I want to do away with everything that is criticized in mass evangelism. We believe it is a spiritual service. We don't believe it is a contest or a sham. Very rarely do I find an atheist. People aren't so smart-alecky anymore. They're scared."

And he added: "America has only three or four years at the most and then it will all be over and we will fall as Rome fell and Germany fell."

The converts who had given Billy Graham so much headline publicity found themselves faced with an entirely new life-style. They too were scared.

They didn't have it easy.

Zamperini tried to get back on his feet, but found little encouragement anywhere. The only help he got was from his wife. He underwent periods of depression and the recurrence of doubts that laid him low several times.

Gradually, however, he began to rebuild his life. He found that nobody really wanted an athlete past his prime. He held several jobs, but they came to nothing.

Then suddenly he got an idea how he could use his athletic accomplishments to good effect. He worked his way into social services. There he found that delinquent boys openly admired athletes, even those put out to pasture. He used his own past prowess as an example for them. They respected him; they loved him. He has worked in that field ever since.

As for Stuart Hamblen, he was fired from his cushy thousand-dollar-a-week radio program when he refused to advertise beer on the air.

"I don't want guys who believe in me to become drunks!" he protested to the studio brass. "I know what it's like to be a lush." His protests did no good. He was out of work.

A friend of his, actor John Wayne, for whom he had done riding stunts at one time, heard he had not taken a drink in thirty days.

"Tell me, Stuart, have you wanted a drink?"

"No, Duke," Hamblen replied. "It is no secret what God can do."

Wayne mused on that. "Well then, why don't you write a song? 'It is no secret what God can do.'"

Hamblen did. The song was a hit. He wrote more in the same vein: "This Old House," "Oh, His Hands." They all did well. He had found a new career.

As a recent admirer said after meeting him for the first time: "The words don't match the face!"

Life had changed for Billy Graham, too. On the train to Minneapolis he and Ruth found that they had become instant celebrities—public "personalities." The conductor treated them like a pair of movie stars.

"The work has been God's and not man's," Billy told the clamoring newsmen. "I want no credit or glory. I want the Lord Jesus to have it all."

The next scheduled engagement of the Graham team was in Boston, a campaign that had been agreed on back in 1947. But Billy was too tired to pitch into the advance work. He was put under a doctor's care and sent home to Montreat to rest and regain his strength.

Billy was scared of Boston. If Los Angeles had given him a lift, Boston could certainly put him down quickly. It was a Roman Catholic stronghold, with minorities of Unitarians and Christian Scientists, none of them particularly friendly to evangelism.

Besides that, it was an intellectual city, a historical city, a proud city. The Evangelical Ministerial Association there considered Billy Graham some kind of untested fledgling upstart.

Several meetings were scheduled at two sites: one meeting at Mechanics Hall, and others at Park Street Congregational Church. The latter was called "Brimstone Corner," since gunpowder was stored there during the Revolution.

From the first, Billy's Los Angeles publicity proved effective in opening doors in Boston. The first night, a hundred and seventy-five people came forward at the call. Dr. Harold Ockenga, who had invited Billy to Boston, said that it was the first time Boston had brought out so many converts in a very long time.

Ockenga booked Mechanics Hall again for Sunday afternoon. It was filled to bursting, with two more halls nearby taking on the hundreds who had been turned away. New Year's Day was being celebrated on Monday —Sunday was really January 1—and the church was packed. Seven thousand people had to be shut out! To add to the confusion, it was pouring rain. Yet over a thousand half-drowned diehards waited in the street outside, singing hymns under their umbrellas.

Billy took over Mechanics Hall for a full week, then the Boston Opera House for four days after. The stunned press ran front-page stories, reporters and editors alike amazed at the heavy, serious-minded crowds.

It was chaos in the suite where the Billy Graham team was working. The hotel telephone operator almost had a nervous breakdown. The board was flooded with long-distance calls for Billy. Upstairs, Grady Wilson was picking out words on a borrowed typewriter with his own hunt-and-peck system, trying to bat out a release covering the newsmen's questions.

What was worse, there was really nowhere else to go. All the usual halls were booked for other events. Yet the crowds kept increasing. It was a definite impasse.

Ockenga suddenly got a call from the editor of the Boston *Post*. "Why don't you book Boston Garden?" he asked. It was a large indoor sports arena, where ice hockey games and other spectacles were held. It seated thirteen thousand. "You think Billy can fill it?"

Ockenga didn't know, but he certainly would try to find out.

Later, when Billy telephoned to thank the editor, who happened to be a devout Roman Catholic, the newsman laughed and admitted: "I don't know why I'm giving you this kind of coverage, or even this kind of good advice—but good luck."

Billy Graham knew the reason why. The Lord was working.

On Monday, January 16, sixteen thousand people squeezed into Boston Garden, leaving so many outside that Billy delivered an unscheduled address from the steps.

After the services ended, the Grahams were whisked off to catch a train for Canada, where Billy had an engagement in Toronto.

There was only one sour note to the New England triumph.

As the train pounded across Massachusetts, Billy felt that he had left his work undone in Boston. Why not get off the train at Worcester and telephone Boston that he would stay for more services?

He did not follow the impulse.

Yet it came to him again the next day. He had invitations from universities, schools, cities and towns all over New England. He could stay for six months, perhaps start a true religious revival.

Billy was tired. He was frightened. Things were happening too fast.

According to John Pollock's official biography: "He now believes that 'unwittingly I disobeyed the voice of God.' "

# CHAPTER TEN

## *Hour of Decision*

After Boston and a short stay in Canada, the Billy Graham team moved to Columbia, South Carolina, for a series of meetings.

To help in the advance work for the campaign, Billy secured the services of a personal friend, Willis Haymaker. The secretary of the Laymen's Evangelistic Clubs of North Carolina, Haymaker was an old hand at organizing campaigns. He had been advance man for Gypsy Smith, Bob Jones and many other famed evangelists of the 1920s.

After Columbia, Billy made him a permanent member of the Graham team.

His influence was felt immediately. He changed the whole concept of Billy's meetings by calling them "crusades" instead of "campaigns." A *crusade* was a continuing thing, he felt. A *campaign* was merely part of a crusade.

"A crusade goes on and on," he said, "and is worldwide in its ramifications."

Billy liked the idea. It widened his own horizons and introduced the concept of deepening his ministry into a global religious movement.

The Columbia Crusade began on Sunday, February 19. On March 1, Billy Graham spoke to a joint meeting of the South Carolina state legislature. Statesman Bernard Baruch read a news report of the meeting at his home in Georgetown, Washington. He called it to the attention of a house guest, Henry R. Luce. Luce

decided to fly down to attend Billy Graham's meeting
on Thursday, March 9. He wired Billy to expect him.

Billy had already announced his sermon as one on
judgment and hell, which he would describe in graphic
detail.

And that wouldn't do for a worldly, well-read intellectual like Luce. He would think it corny and ridiculous. Billy was tempted to change the subject. If he
sounded like a two-bit preacher to Luce, he might lose
all the good press he had been getting.

After meditation and prayer, Billy went right to
Scripture. God's words to Jeremiah, 1:17, were: "Thou
therefore gird up thy loins, and arise, and speak unto
them all that I command thee: be not dismayed at their
faces, lest I confound thee before them."

The message was clear to Billy. If he changed his
style, God would put him down in front of his audience. The intent of the verse was *not* to compromise.

He did not. At the call, two hundred and fifty-six
people came forward. Later on, Henry Luce invited
Billy Graham to the executive mansion, where he was
staying. The two men chatted easily and formed a
friendship that endured to Luce's death.

Next day a *Life* team flew to Columbia and took
pictures at the outdoor stadium where thirty-five thousand heard Billy speak a sermon on Noah and the
flood. The *Life* spread of the event reached many
millions of people who had never heard of Billy.

By the summer of 1950 the Billy Graham team had
added a few new faces and had begun to take on a more
distinctive and definite shape.

Grady Wilson had been with the team almost from
the beginning. So had Cliff Barrows, with his trombone
and his voice. Likewise, George Beverly Shea. And
Willis Haymaker was a newcomer with priceless qualifi-
cations.

At Northwestern Schools in 1950 before he resigned,
Billy had a staff composed of George Wilson, in charge
of the school; T. W. Wilson, Grady's brother, vice-

president; and Luverne Gustavson and Betty Lowry, secretaries.

Another member of the staff was Gerald Beavan, a young Baptist minister, who had joined Northwestern's faculty just before Riley's death.

Billy made him registrar. Although he liked the young man's work, Billy did not really know him well. After the Los Angeles rally and before leaving for Boston in 1949, Billy was talking to Beavan one day when the young man said:

"I'd give my right arm to go with you to Boston."

Billy raised an eyebrow.

"I might be able to handle the press," Beavan suggested.

During the confused press situation in Boston, Billy remembered his brief conversation with Beavan. Now, after Columbia, with another New England swing scheduled, he sent for Beavan and made him his press secretary.

Jerry Beavan proved worthy of the job, protecting Billy from difficult press questions and from off-the-cuff remarks that might hurt his image.

Beavan had a flair for organization. He was also a quick study when it came to assessing difficult situations. Along with Grady Wilson and Willis Haymaker, he handled the phone calls and complaints that kept coming in. He soon showed a born talent for sorting out muddles, smoothing ruffled feelings and protecting Billy from those who wanted to put him on the spot.

But even Beavan could make a mistake.

On July 14 Billy Graham was invited to meet President Truman at the White House. The invitation was proof that Billy had arrived nationally. Through the help of the press, he was now known as a religious figure. He was one step from being a "household name."

Grady Wilson and Jerry Beavan accompanied him to the White House. At the end of an interesting twenty-minute chat, the President rose, signifying the end of the interview. Billy asked if they might pray.

"Well," said Truman, "I don't suppose any harm could be done by that."

They did so, and the Graham team left.

On the White House lawn they were surrounded by newsmen. The press pushed at Billy so hard he inadvertently revealed that he and his team had prayed with the President. Without realizing it, he violated protocol by telling the press exactly what had happened.

Photographers persuaded him and his team to pray on the lawn. Every newspaper in the country carried the picture.

Mr. Truman never invited him to the White House again.

Shortly after that, a big and important turning point came into the life of Billy Graham.

It was the death of Walter A. Maier. Maier was *the* evangelical preacher in America, the founder and weekly radio preacher of *The Lutheran Hour*, "Bringing Christ to the Nations."

His death brought up the problem of a worthy successor in the prestigious radio ministry. Dr. Theodore Elsner, president of National Religious Broadcasters, the man in charge of *The Lutheran Hour*, was staying that week in Ocean City, New Jersey, with his son-in-law, Fred Dienert, an advertising agency executive from Philadelphia.

Elsner knew he had to find someone of stature to take Maier's place on the program very soon. He thought of Billy Graham. Suddenly, he was hungry for breakfast. There was no food at the cottage where he was staying. He drove out to find a lunch counter. At Somers Point he saw a roadside diner, stopped and went in.

Coincidentally, Billy Graham and Cliff Barrows were attending an Ocean City religious conference. That same morning they played golf with a friend and then stopped at the same diner to eat.

Elsner recognized Billy, introduced himself and immediately launched into a plea for him to take on the radio program.

Billy was amused. "How am I going to get on national radio? Who's going to help me?"

Elsner said that his son-in-law, Fred Dienert, was a junior partner of Walter F. Bennett of Chicago. Their advertising agency, the Walter Bennett Advertising Company, had promoted and arranged *The Lutheran Hour*.

"No," said Billy. He pointed out that a national program could be a full-time job. He had his Crusades to worry about.

Elsner left, saddened that his idea had not taken root the way he had wanted it to.

Four weeks later, Walter F. Bennett and Fred Dienert introduced themselves to Billy Graham during a conference in northern Michigan. They tried to persuade Billy to take over the radio show, but he turned them down.

Later on they approached him at Montreat. There they told him that a peak Sunday-afternoon time slot would be available coast-to-coast on the ABC network, with an initial thirteen-week contract going at ninety-two thousand dollars.

No deal, said Billy. The sum was too staggering even to consider.

A six-week Graham Crusade began in Portland, Oregon. The ubiquitous Bennett and Dienert team besieged Billy by telephone and telegraph, explaining the financing of the program at seven thousand dollars a week. If Billy raised an initial twenty-five thousand dollars, he could go on the air. After three weeks the gifts of listeners would maintain the cost: so said Bennett and Dienert.

Following up their telegrams and calls, Bennett and Dienert appeared in Portland. Billy was getting fed up with these hard-sell promoters. He refused to see them. The two ad men left.

They reappeared ten days later.

Billy was forced to enter and leave the Multnomah Hotel by the rear elevator. Once he even went down the fire escape while they camped out in the lobby.

They waited a week. Their persistence finally paid off. Billy gave them an appointment. The appointment, amusingly enough, coincided with Billy Graham's rest-and-recreation trip to Mount Hood.

In the middle of breakfast at Mount Hood, a phone call came in for Billy from an old friend in Texas who owned a grocery chain.

"I hear you want to go on the radio, Billy."

Billy frowned. He thought he detected the fine Italian hand of Bennett and Dienert.

"I've got a buddy in the bakery business who wants to go in with me to start a fund for you. We'll each ante up a thousand dollars."

Next morning when he got back from Mount Hood, Billy saw the ad men waiting for him in the hotel lobby. He went in the back way and lay down to rest. The pair got through to Grady Wilson. Wilson told Billy that the two had scheduled a flight back home that night and wouldn't bother him anymore.

Billy relented and agreed to see them.

He was pacing up and down in the hotel room when Bennett and Dienert came in. Biographer John Pollock described Billy as clad in pajamas and golf cap. "He always wore the golf cap to keep his hair from getting unruly when he lay down," Pollock explained.

"I still haven't decided," Billy told the two men. "However, I do have an offer of two thousand dollars from friends of mine."

Bennett and Dienert nodded.

"I suppose I could contact other wealthy men. I just don't have the time. That's why I've been keeping out of your way."

The two ad men smiled. "You've been doing a good job of it," Bennett conceded.

"Billy," Dienert said, "I don't think the money is going to come from a lot of big people."

Bennett agreed. "I think you should tell your Portland audience about the show and see what they do."

Billy continued pacing and thinking. Finally he turned on them, with a smile. "Boys, let's pray."

He got on his knees, and the two ad men joined him beside the bed. Billy began explaining things to God. He explained the problem and pointed out how difficult it was to raise twenty-five thousand dollars.

Then, as at Los Angeles, Billy asked God to give him a sign. And what a sign it was this time!

Fred Dienert later recalled the words of Billy's prayer to biographer Pollock:

"Lord, You know I'm doing all that I can. You know I don't have any money, but I believe we ought to do this. You know, Lord, I have a mortgage on that little house in Montreat. Lord, I'll put another mortgage on; I'll take the little I have and put another mortgage on.

"Lord, I don't know where the money is, and if I did know where it is, I'm too busy to go out and get it.

"I feel the burden for it, but it's up to You, and if You want this, I want You to give me a sign. And I'm going to put out the fleece. And the fleece is for the twenty-five thousand dollars by *midnight.*"

Astounded at the enormity of Billy Graham's faith, the two ad men retreated from the hotel suite and took a cab to the airport.

On the way out, they began talking. Each had the feeling that something was going to happen. They had sensed the urgency of the prayer that Billy Graham had given. They thought it would be answered.

Checking their bags, they took another cab back to the Crusade, seating themselves in the far rear. They could see that a huge crowd, about twenty thousand, had come. That was a good harbinger. If Billy mentioned the sum when the plates were passed, the take might approximate twenty-five thousand dollars.

All the way up to the offering, Billy did not mention the radio program. The two ad men were puzzled and quite unhappy.

Only after the offering had been collected did Billy tell the audience about the radio program. He said that he did indeed hope to do the radio show. He pointed out, however, that he did not have enough money to put it on, nor did he have the time to go about and raise backing.

"If any of you folks would like to have a part in this undertaking, I'll be in the office back here at the close of the service tonight."

He mentioned the sum he needed: twenty-five thousand dollars. There were a few nervous titters in the audience.

To the two advertising men, the sermon and the guest address which followed seemed extremely protracted, and the call for decisions for Christ seemed interminable.

Finally Billy left the podium. A line began forming at the back office. Inside, Grady Wilson held an old shoe box. Offerings came in, in bills, in IOUs, in pledges.

A lumberman from Idaho left a twenty-five-hundred-dollar pledge. A woman in a black dress extended a five-dollar bill, saying that it was all she had. Others threw in quarters and dimes. A businessman pledged one thousand dollars.

Then Billy caught sight of Bennett and Dienert and smiled at them. When the line thinned out, Grady Wilson handed over the box of money and IOUs to the Crusade chairman for counting. The team went out to Louie's-on-the-Alley for oyster stew. Bennett and Dienert joined them.

At the end of the meal the Crusade chairman entered the oyster bar excitedly. The total take, including the promised $2,000 from Texas, was just $23,500.

Everybody looked at Billy.

"It's a miracle," one of them said. "You're as good as on the air!"

Billy, astounded and almost in tears at the fantastic generosity and the trust of the people who had come to see him, slowly shook his head.

"No. The fleece was for twenty-five thousand dollars before midnight. It's got to be twenty-five thousand dollars, or where's God's word? The devil might be sending us a lesser sum to tempt us."

Bennett and Dienert offered to put up the balance, but Billy refused to accept it.

Subdued, the team returned to the Multnomah Hotel shortly before midnight. Billy went to his room. On the way up after him, Grady Wilson stopped at the desk to collect whatever mail there was. He was handed three envelopes that had been delivered personally.

In each was a pledge from somebody who had been unable to wait in line and had brought his offering directly to the hotel.

The first envelope had two hundred and fifty dollars in it. The second also had two hundred and fifty dollars in it.

The third envelope had a pledge for one thousand dollars.

Together they made up the difference between the original sum and twenty-five thousand dollars.

That night Grady Wilson kept the shoe box in his shirt drawer. When he took it to the bank the next morning, he learned that if he entered the cash and the checks under his name he would be liable for income tax on the total amount. He learned also that it could not go in tax-free under "Billy Graham Radio Fund," because that "group" was not a properly constituted body or corporation.

Grady put the money into the account of the Portland Crusade, a tax-free organization.

Billy immediately called George Wilson at Northwestern Schools in Minneapolis and spelled out the problem. Wilson caught the next flight out to the Coast, bringing with him articles of incorporation for the Billy Graham Evangelistic Association, which he had already drawn up against just such an eventuality.

Billy, Ruth, Cliff, Grady Wilson and George Wilson became the officers of the corporation. The money for the radio program could now be used to pay for the air time. As yet the program had no name. It was Ruth who came up with *Hour of Decision,* which they liked better than Billy's proposed *Decision for Christ.*

While all this activity was going on out in Portland, the ABC top brass met and killed the program.

When Bennett arrived in the network offices in Chicago to sign the contract as arranged by telephone, he was told that the New York brass had changed their minds and would not sell the time to Billy Graham.

Bennett and Dienert flew to New York immediately. It was Saturday. No one was around. However, a vice-president who had missed the board meeting came in unexpectedly while they were there.

After a lengthy discussion, the two advertising men persuaded the vice-president to call another meeting. The vice-president phoned one of the top executives, who was on a Westchester golf course, and set up a meeting for Monday.

Two days later the board decided unanimously that the program should go on.

# CHAPTER ELEVEN

# The Association

On November 5, 1950, *Hour of Decision* was broadcast over one hundred and fifty stations on the ABC radio network. The program originated in Georgia, where the Graham team had gone for the Atlanta Crusade.

The program format was simple. Cliff Barrows introduced the show and then led the choir and the audience in songs. Jerry Beavan gave a short summary of the news. Grady Wilson read selections from Scripture. George Beverly Shea sang a group of songs. Then Billy Graham came on.

Although his associates and friends had always advised Billy to speak slowly and quietly on the air, as a contrast to his rapid-fire, hard-hitting diction at the pulpit, he rejected the advice when he appeared on national network radio. He had made a careful study of successful news commentators and newscasters and had found that those with rapid delivery—for example Walter Winchell and Drew Pearson—got the most listeners.

He intended his weekly sermon to cover as much ground as possible, including social and political issues as well as religious illustrations and Bible quotations.

Using his swift, rattling diction, he began the first show with a report on the Chinese intervention in the Korean War. Then he spoke of those who blamed Christianity for the world's ills, pointing out that the Christian faith was based on peace, not bloodshed.

"Faith, more than fighting, can change the course of

events today," he said. "United, believing, self-humbling, God-exalting prayer now can change the course of history."

In five weeks *Hour of Decision*—which was actually a half-hour show—had earned the highest audience ever achieved by a religious presentation. Within five years it was being heard on a total of eight hundred and fifty stations on a worldwide basis, three hundred and fifty of them in North America. By 1970 it was heard on over nine hundred stations.

Letters began pouring in—178,726 the first year, 362,545 the second, and each year the number rose steadily. Four years later the Minneapolis office of the Billy Graham Evangelistic Association had eighty employees rather than the two with which it had started.

In fact, the Association, created to solve a problem in funding, eventually became the heart and soul of the Billy Graham movement. George Wilson, secretary-treasurer of the BGEA at its inception, was eventually forced to take on the job as a full-time affair.

The launching of the radio show had once again raised the thorny problem of collections, which had been a major source of trouble from the start for Billy Graham. Up to the time of the creation of the Association, Billy had accepted donations from friends, collections during services and honorariums offered by organizations or sponsors. He had split the money in most cases with his associates.

In addition, he was paid a regular salary for his work at Northwestern Schools. And he was paid for his work with Youth for Christ during the war and the early postwar years.

The problem had not yet been solved. With the radio program reaching millions of people, many of whom might wish to donate money to the cause of Christ, Billy was worried that the public might get the mistaken idea that evangelism was a money-making racket and nothing more. Actually, sophisticated cynics had always believed it *was* a racket. In fact, some evangelists *had* made it a lucrative payoff.

On the first radio program Cliff Barrows ended the show with a very soft-sell suggestion:

"Now, we're looking to you, our listening audience, for the encouragement your letters will bring."

Envelopes were then passed out to the Atlanta audience, to be mailed to Billy Graham in Minneapolis.

In addition, on the last night of the six-week Crusade, a "love offering" was given by the audience, and when it was totaled up, Billy Graham was staggered at the amount. It was a great deal more than he had anticipated.

Two photos were printed on the front page of the Atlanta *Constitution* the next day. One showed Billy Graham waving a farewell to Atlanta as he boarded a train. The other showed ushers holding up four enormous money bags. The pictures told the story. Even if unintended, it was a beautiful hatchet job.

Billy Graham was now a national figure, a media personality, and the country's most visible advocate of the Christian way of life. The moral implications of the newspaper pictures could well destroy all the good his evangelism had produced so far.

He and his aides decided something must be done about the gathering, distribution and spending of the money. The entire transaction, from start to finish, Billy decided, had to be clean, clear-cut and aboveboard. There could be no hint that the members of the Graham team were lining their pockets with the money.

Jesse Bader, secretary of Evangelism for the National Council of Churches, suggested that Billy use the Association he had created.

"Pay yourself a salary and don't take love offerings and you can make history in evangelism," Bader said. "You can lift evangelism to a place of confidence and high regard in America that it has not had since D. L. Moody."

Billy Graham followed Bader's suggestion. The last love offering was taken in 1951. A few months later he stopped taking honorariums. The only collections taken were channeled to pay for the radio show, *Hour of*

*Decision.* The money not needed for the show was set aside to pay for advance work on new Crusades. The Graham team never did believe in pinching pennies for religious enterprises.

An aide once said, "Too much work done in the name of Christ is run-down, baggy-trousers stuff. Billy believes in going first class."

And anyway, as Billy once neatly pointed out, "Most Crusades cost less than the sum earned by a champion boxer in one big fight!"

Why not promote religion as heavily as sports? "As long as the money is not going into our private pockets, and as long as our motives are right before God, I see no reason why we cannot spend almost any amount in order to reach a city for Christ."

When the Billy Graham Evangelistic Association was formed, Billy paid himself $15,000 a year through the Association. With inflation and the rise in the cost of living, the sum has risen proportionately through the years. In 1973, for example, it was $24,500, well within the bounds of the inflationary spiral.

The salaries of the other members of the Graham team, as well as the BGEA employees in Minneapolis, were paid through the same system.

Only one separate source of income did Billy allow for himself—the proceeds from the sales of his books, which now number thirteen. Royalties from some of the books did not go directly to him, either. The income was set aside as a trust fund for the education of his five children.

The Association began in a three-room office with one employee and George Wilson. It is now a multi-million-dollar complex presided over by the same man who formed it and ran it in the beginning—George Wilson.

Alan Bestic, a British writer, interviewed Wilson for his book *Praise the Lord and Pass the Contribution.*

"Wilson, a short, plump, happy man in his middle fifties, is ideal for the job and properly proud that he can keep both God and Caesar well serviced," he wrote.

"I started here with a staff of one twenty-six years ago," Wilson told Bestic. "Now we have more than three hundred and fifty, working three shifts round the clock and I still find time to do a bit of lay preaching. I suppose I could have gone into business, but what would I have made, except money?

"I don't have a lot of that now, but there's nothing I need that I haven't got. I've no ulcer department. I've never had an ache or a pain in a quarter of a century. All that—and the pleasure of seeing people's lives change."

The Association has grown into a vast conglomerate of printing and publishing departments, filing and mailing sections, spiritual counselors' offices, a chapel, a cinema and dozens of computers.

According to biographer John Pollock, Billy Graham turned down three film offers that could have made him rich. He also refused an ABC network television offer that would have netted him over one million dollars a year. Clearly, his fame and his abilities would make him the perfect candidate for any company's board of directors. He has been urged to get into politics, but he has refused.

Alan Bestic concluded: "I think that it is fair to say that he does not seek excessive wealth, merely the comfortable living which he earns by working extremely hard."

The Association is involved in a number of other projects ancillary to evangelism. A staff was set up to answer the many hundreds of letters received every week from listeners. Most of these communications contain no money, but are written by people seeking spiritual guidance. The epistles come from all kinds of people in all conditions of life. The Association tries to answer the letters promptly, and does not solicit funds when responding.

The staff of women who read this "problem mail" begin their day's proceedings—before they have read a letter—with a special "season of prayer" in which, as one of them explained to biographer Stanley High, "We ask God to give us understanding and wisdom in classifying this mail and suggesting how it can be answered."

Billy Graham discovered upon analysis that the mail tends to fall into about forty definite categories. The substance of a reply for the problem in each of the categories has been prepared, given a number and entered in a computer, and can be run off by pressing a button. The computer then prints the letter, seals it and sends it on its way.

However, a personalized introduction and conclusion for each letter is written by an associate of George Wilson.

Not all letters fall into specific categories. For example:

> My wife and I will doubtless go to Heaven. We have been married, and peacefully, for many years. We are nearly sixty and are almost typical. We sort of mind our own affairs, never cause anyone any trouble. My problem—I just can't imagine spending an eternity with my wife. One hundred thousand years or so, yes. But eternity—well I just don't see how I can stand it. Isn't there some way I could avoid going to Heaven and at the same time not go to Hell?

There is no record of how that one was answered.

In spite of the careful way in which the Graham team has managed its collections, there is still some honest skepticism among the press and the cynical as to "hidden funds," "laundered money" and the like.

Each Crusade is audited by a local firm. The audit is published in newspapers at the end of the Crusade.

In Los Angeles during the last days of the 1949 campaign, Billy Graham met a film producer named Dick Ross. Ross had been production manager for Moody Institute of Science films. He then owned a small production company called Great Commission Films.

Billy invited him to make a documentary of the upcoming Portland campaign. When the film was made, it contained a memorable scene with Cliff Barrows acting out for schoolchildren the cleansing of Naaman in the River Jordan—"Seven Ducks in Muddy Water."

Later in March 1951 Ross made a feature picture for Billy, a story about a cowboy who is converted to God. Called *Mr. Texas,* it was shown all over the country, although *Variety* called it "off-beat and amateurish." The show-biz paper predicted: "Will find an audience only on the religious circuit and even there may be limited to Billy Graham converts."

In 1951 World Wide Pictures was incorporated to produce and distribute Billy Graham films. The second picture, *Oiltown, U.S.A.,* was made in 1952. After that, several films a year were produced by World Wide Pictures, all with religious themes of an evangelistic nature. Many were successful not only on the church circuit but in big movie houses as well.

In December 1952 Billy Graham also broke into print, with a regular daily feature called "My Answer," distributed by the Chicago Tribune–New York News Syndicate. In 1973 it went to two hundred newspapers with combined circulations of twenty-two million.

His first big-selling book, *Peace with God,* was published in 1953 by Doubleday, and has sold over one and a quarter million copies in English alone. Over two million copies have been sold worldwide in various languages.

Other books he has written include: *Calling Youth to Christ, Revival in Our Time, America's Hour of Decision, Secret of Happiness, Seven Deadly Sins, World Aflame, The Challenge: Sermons from Madison Square Garden* and *Angels: God's Secret Agents.*

# CHAPTER TWELVE

# Evangelism

By 1950 Billy Graham had become a household name and had even been invited to attend the White House to meet the President. It was obvious to the public that America was moving into a brand-new phase of religious revival.

The postwar years brought with them a scramble to make and buy more consumer goods and to create more physical comfort for the American consumer. And yet, with the push for creature comforts, there was an inner, unexpressed desire to make some kind of sense out of America's heritage. It was a time of trying to get it all together inside as well as outside.

Counselors and authors were producing philosophical works stressing inner tranquility and telling Americans how they could build new, happy lives in the postwar world amid the materialism and the stress of commercial competition. The idea was for man to cooperate with God to build better communities

To the intelligent American, the Cold War and its political tensions made such appeals for "cooperation" a bit ridiculous. No one was really fooled or taken in by the idea that he could lift himself up by his bootstraps.

It became obvious that more than cooperation was needed—perhaps a more radical transformation of the psyche. It was to this end that the evangelistic messages of Billy Graham were directed. And the public was willing to listen.

The typical evangelistic message was simple: Only

if man realized his inadequacy, his sins and his in-
ability to change himself and the world in which he
lived, only if he turned completely to Christ, could
he be forgiven, made new and filled with God's spirit.
Then, armed with this new strength, he might conquer
his inner turmoil and be able to live more at peace with
God and his fellow man.

"The evangelistic message so central to Graham's
ministry was similar to that of the great revivalists
Moody and Sunday, but Graham was to build a larger,
more inclusive and longer-lasting constituency than
these earlier evangelists," wrote Lowell D. Streiker and
Gerald S. Strober in *Religion and the New Majority*.

The kind of evangelism practiced by the tent revivalists with whom Billy Graham had been familiar
in his youth actually came from a long and honorable
line of religious endeavor. Historically, evangelism
flourished in both England and the United States many
years before the dawn of the twentieth century.

The word "evangelism" itself, of course, goes back
even further.

"Evangelist" comes from the Greek for "gospel," and
the word means someone who preaches the Gospel. The
original evangelists in the Bible were Matthew, Mark,
Luke and John.

In the modern sense, the term refers to Protestant
preachers who go about the country or countryside
preaching personal conversion to religion.

Historically, the most significant effort of evangelism
was undoubtedly the Great Awakening, a dynamic
revival in interest in soul conversion that took place in
the eighteenth century in America.

It comprised a series of religious revivals that swept
over the American Colonies in the middle of the eighteenth century. It resulted in many changes in church
doctrine and exerted a strong influence on social and
political thought in the colonies.

It began in New Jersey under the evangelical preachings of Theodorus Frelinghuysen of the Dutch Reformed
Church and Gilbert Tennent of the Presbyterian de-

nomination. Tennent became the leading figure of the
Great Awakening in the Middle Colonies.

In New England the revival in religious interest was
started by the revivalist preaching of Jonathan Edwards
of Northampton.

Attracted to the ferment of religious stirrings, preachers came over from England, among them John Wesley, founder of Methodism, and George Whitefield,
one of the most famous preachers of his day. Soon
all the isolated rivulets of revivalism united and began
flowering in one steady stream through all the colonies.

The revival reached the South with the preaching of
Samuel Davies among the Presbyterians of Virginia.
Later it spread to the Baptists in North Carolina in the
1760s. Finally, just before the American Revolution,
a rapid spread of Methodism occurred.

Along with a revived interest in preaching, the Great
Awakening resulted in an outburst of missionary effort.
This was accompanied by the first movement of any
importance in America against slavery. Other humani-
tarian undertakings were instituted, including the spread
of education and learning. It led to the founding of a
number of academies and colleges, among them Princeton, Brown, Rutgers and Dartmouth.

The religious revival served to build up interests
that were intercolonial in character, strengthening the
separate sections that were to become the United States
of America. It increased opposition to the Anglican
Church and to the Royalist officials who supported it.
The revival actually created a democratic spirit in religion that was allied with the insistence of the colonies
on political home rule.

While the nature of the evangelist movement in
England was revolutionary, in America it was even
more animated and attended by a great deal of emotional excitement and physical manifestation.

In 1797 James McGready had already begun to hold
outdoor meetings in Kentucky, which soon grew into
the type of congregations later called camp meetings.

After McGready, Asathel Nettleton and Charles

Grandison Finney continued the evangelistic work in the eastern United States up to 1850.

But it was Dwight L. Moody who, with the singing evangelist Ira D. Sankey, roused audiences to religious fervor for more than twenty-five years at the beginning of the nineteenth century. They set the tone of the peculiarly American version of English evangelism.

Modern English evangelism started with John Wesley, who with his brother Charles founded the Methodist Church. John Wesley, born in Epworth, Lincolnshire, in 1703, was ordained a deacon in the Church of England in 1725, elected a fellow of Lincoln College, Oxford, in 1726 and ordained a priest in 1728.

At Oxford in 1729, he took the lead in a dissident group of religious students gathered around his younger brother Charles. They were derisively called "Methodists" by their enemies because of their "methodical" devotion to study and to religious duties.

In 1735 the Wesleys accompanied political leader James Oglethorpe to Georgia, where John was to serve as a religious missionary among the Indians and Charles was to act as secretary to Oglethorpe. John stayed in America only two years. He became interested in the Moravian missionaries he met in the colony of Georgia.

On his return to England, at a meeting of a small religious society in Aldersgate Street, London, on May 24, 1738, Wesley experienced an "assurance of salvation" through faith in Christ alone. It was his true conversion to Christianity, the evangelist's crossing over to work for Christ. His conviction in Christianity formed the basis of his message to the world for the rest of his life.

Wesley entered upon a career of evangelistic work which lasted all his life. In the course of it he preached some forty thousand sermons and traveled a quarter of a million miles on horseback. Historians called his faithfully kept journal a "guidebook" of England.

Soon all church doors had been shut to him by the Anglican Church. The Establishment had repudiated him because of his interest in the Moravian cult, and because of his loudly proclaimed "conversion." Unable to preach indoors, he began open-air or field preaching after the fashion of his friend and close associate George Whitefield.

In 1739 a group in London asked him to help them form a religious society and act as their leader. He agreed to do so. They bought an old abandoned foundry at Moorfields, which remained the center of Methodist work in London until 1778.

In 1784 Wesley issued a declaration by which the Methodist societies became legally constituted. In essence, this became the charter of the Wesleyan Methodists.

Wesley insisted that each individual was a responsible object of God's interest, and that each ought to develop a healthy mind and healthy body as well as a devoted heart. The hymns he translated were among the earliest importations of the spirit of European Romanticism.

John's brother Charles Wesley was always a close associate, and led his own congregations in singing the hymns John had written and translated.

George Whitefield joined the Methodist group started by the Wesley brothers when he entered Oxford in 1732. Ordained a deacon in the Church of England in 1736, he soon became an excellent and compelling preacher, not only because of his voice and his appearance but also because of his obvious ability in dramatics and stagecraft.

Whitefield made the first of seven trips to America in 1738. He spent a short time in Georgia in the mission post just vacated by John Wesley. On his return to England to seek funds for an orphanage in Georgia, he was ordained an Anglican priest.

However, his connection with the Wesleys and the evangelical character of his preaching led to his later exclusion from most of the pulpits of the Church of England. He continued to preach where he was invited, and where he wasn't, he began holding meetings in the open air.

Huge audiences were attracted to these outdoor congregations. He was a preaching evangelist who could address thousands in the open air and command rapt attention from them all. It was he who persuaded John Wesley to carry on in open-air work after Wesley was similarly shut out by the Anglican Church.

He visited America again in 1740 and became an influential figure in the Great Awakening, preaching to congregations in the settlements from Georgia to New England. He joined in and helped stimulate the Great Revival in progress in America, visiting his friend Jonathan Edwards, who had started a revival in 1736 in Northampton, Massachusetts.

In addition to America, Whitefield preached in Scotland, Wales and England. It was his custom to preach at least three or four times a day. He was founder and chief supporter of an orphanage in Oglethorpe, Georgia, and a nationally known figure. He helped unite the people of the American colonies, for he was known from New England to Georgia.

Theologically he was a Calvinist. He was not primarily an organizer, but a man of profound experience, and he was able to communicate this living experience through clear expression infused with passion.

His last sermon was delivered in the open air at Exeter, Massachusetts, in 1770, and he died in Newburyport, Massachusetts, where he is buried.

It was out of the open-air meetings of Wesley and Whitefield that the American version, called the "camp meeting," evolved. In America the preaching of James McGready in Kentucky in the course of the religious revival around 1800 used open-air meetings with great success, and that type of evangelistic preaching spread to the West as the movement grew and the West opened up.

On the frontier there was no indoor place to hold large meetings. Because of the absence of halls and buildings, the people came from miles around to the fields and prairies where the traveling revival preachers were scheduled to conduct meetings.

Visitors brought bedding and provisions in order to

camp for several days right on the grounds where the revivals were to take place.

To combat inclement weather, tents were sometimes set up to cover altar and pulpit. If the mud became too sticky, sawdust was spread around to lay it. The term "sawdust trail" became recognized as an apt descriptive phrase for the revivalist, evangelistic type of camp meeting and tent-revival ceremony.

As the meetings developed they were directed by a number of preachers who relieved one another in carrying on the services or preached simultaneously in different parts of the campgrounds. Shouting, shaking and rolling on the ground frequently accompanied the tremendous emotional release that followed the conversions.

Though these extravagances were opposed and discouraged by conservative ministers, they continued to grow in popularity among the people of the western frontier.

Camp meetings were usually held by evangelical sects, like the Methodists, the Baptists and the Cumberland Presbyterians. Other new denominations developed out of the religious revival.

In modified form the camp meeting continued to be a feature of social and religious life in the region between the Alleghenies and the Mississippi River until comparatively recent times. In a sense, they survive today in summer conferences and assemblies.

In 1797 George McGready, an American Presbyterian minister and evangelist born in 1758, developed a type of fiery, rousing preaching in Logan County, Kentucky, that kindled the flame of a great religious revival which swept over the South and the West in 1800.

Gatherings encamped for McGready's revivals were the forerunners of the later camp meetings which spread out West. Some of his methods were questioned by the Presbyterian Church.

In the division of the church that resulted, the Cumberland Presbyterian Church was established. Later

McGready was received back into his presbytery and in 1811 was sent to Indiana to found churches there.

Dwight Lymon Moody, a shoe salesman from Boston, became one of the nineteenth century's greatest American evangelists. He left his business in Boston and moved to Chicago, where he met Ira D. Sankey. His business proved so successful that he quit it and devoted himself full time to city missionary work.

Sankey was a singer and composer who had come from Pennsylvania. During his early years Sankey became an evangelist singer and leader, and turned his talents to the composition of hymns.

After they joined forces, he and Moody became inseparable. Moody preached the sermons and Sankey led the singing. They held evangelistic campaigns throughout the United States as well as Canada and Mexico. Among their more notable evangelistic successes were those in Brooklyn, Philadelphia, Baltimore and at the Chicago World's Fair of 1893.

The two men then sailed for Europe and held evangelistic campaigns in Great Britain in 1873–75, 1881–84 and 1891–92. It was said there that the campaigns influenced Britain's religious life more than any movement since that of John and Charles Wesley.

In the United States, Moody opened Northfield Seminary for girls in 1879 and the Mount Hermon School for boys in 1881. The Moody Bible Institute grew out of the Chicago Evangelization Society, begun in 1886. In 1887 Moody originated the great annual Students' Conference at Northfield. These conferences are still yearly gatherings.

He was a conservative in theology, but was able to gather around him the leading evangelical figures of his time. Records show that he raised millions of dollars while retaining no private wealth. He was a tireless worker to the end of his life, trusted by all and free from sectarian bias. He led hundreds of thousands to confess Christ as Savior.

Probably one of the most colorful of all the evangelists of the last century was William Ashley Sunday, better known as Billy Sunday. Sunday was born in Ames, Iowa, on November 18, 1862. He spent his boyhood in two orphanages and worked his way through high school.

He was so good at playing baseball in high school that he soon got a job as a professional ball player with a local team in Marshalltown, Iowa. The big-league teams heard of him, and scouts brought him to Chicago in 1883. For the next decade he played successively on teams in Chicago, Pittsburgh and Philadelphia.

In a Chicago mission, in 1887, he was converted to Christ. After 1891 he devoted himself to religious work exclusively, first in the YMCA and after 1896 as a preacher.

He was a colorful, athletic evangelist, using his body as well as his big voice in his work. Stalking back and forth on the makeshift stages, thundering out over the crowd with warnings of hellfire and brimstone, he would literally scare the wits out of his audiences.

In 1903 he was ordained in the Presbyterian ministry. Using his baseball popularity to create a national image, he rapidly developed into the most widely known evangelist of his time.

He understood all the facets of publicity. He used press conferences wherever he went. He advertised in all the newspapers. He used poster campaigns that practically obliterated the features of towns he visited. He distributed handbills door-to-door. He held street-corner rallies.

There was no type of ballyhoo, no matter how "lowbrow," that he did not utilize. And he created a big, high-powered organization of public relations men—flacks—to carry out his advance work, as well as his appearances.

Church groups were horrified at his excesses. But people came to watch the show, as well as to be wooed by God. In spite of the lifted eyebrows of the conservative church groups, he packed in crowds that made pastors blink. And he got converts, too.

Newspapers carried stories of Billy Sunday, magazines featured him, books were written about him, congressmen printed his sermons in the *Congressional Record*. He was a phenomenon of promotion at the beginning of the communications era.

Estimates later showed that he converted approximately three hundred thousand during his preaching days.

His conversions were only part of his influence. From his early days, Sunday had thundered denunciations against alcohol. He hated saloons as much as Carry Nation did. Loudly and effectively he railed against the evils of liquor and its deadly influence on the workingmen of America. It was principally because of his widely publicized denunciations of liquor that the Eighteenth Amendment was passed by Congress. The "dry" experiment that followed in the United States carried the imprint of Billy Sunday.

With all his high-minded religiosity, Sunday was a clown as well, and would pose for photographers in ludicrous stances. His athletic background gave him the agility and strength to go through long-protracted revival sessions that would have killed a lesser man.

It was said that he played the press as if it were a musical instrument and he a master of melody. Certainly he used every possible publicity pitch then known to make his meetings successful. And he created a memorable image of himself—Billy Sunday—as an evangelist and man of God that was known to every American who ever opened a newspaper or magazine.

He died in Chicago on November 6, 1935.

Evangelists weren't all men. One of the most renowned and noted of them all was a woman—Aimee Semple McPherson. Aimee Kennedy was born on October 9, 1890, in a farmhouse near Ingersoll, Ontario, in Canada. Her father came from a family of ministers and her mother was brought up in the home of a Salvation Army captain and his wife.

At the age of three weeks Aimee accompanied her mother on a local Salvation Army jubilee. At six weeks she was on the platform.

At the age of seventeen years she was so over-whelmed by a revival meeting run by Robert James Semple that she ran off with him. Even before the honeymoon was over they were off on a revival mission tour, with Chicago on the itinerary.

They went to England and then the Orient, where Robert fell ill and died, just a month before Aimee's daughter, Roberta Star, was born.

Back in America, Aimee worked at the missions, then married Harold Stewart McPherson. Bad health caught up with Aimee. Literally at death's door, she rededicated herself to the service of God.

In 1915, Aimee, now known as Sister McPherson, put up a banner, COME TO THE GREAT CAMP MEETING, and began conducting Pentacostal mission services in Canada, assisted by her husband. Her son, Rolf, was born in Rhode Island shortly after their marriage.

Disappointed at the small crowds, she went out to the main street of Kitchener, Ontario, and preached on a street corner like a member of the Salvation Army. A crowd gathered. Aimee led them back to the church like the Pied Piper of Hamlin. The revival boom was on.

In 1918 McPherson decided he had had enough. Aimee went on without him. In the same year, her mother joined her, and the two headed for Los Angeles. From there she and "Ma" Kennedy, as her mother was affectionately called, traveled across the country seven times, preaching all the way. In 1922 she gave the first radio sermon ever broadcast in San Francisco.

In 1921 she laid the cornerstone of the "Angelus Temple" near Echo Park in Los Angeles. Two years later it was completed, and an organ played "Open the Gates of the Temple!" The temple was opened, and Aimee was in business.

From the beginning the temple prospered. Sister Aimee conducted twenty-one services every week. In 1924 she started the radio broadcasts on her own radio station KFSG.

All was not smooth in the life of the female evangelist. After loud criticism from Los Angeles clergymen, particularly the conservative Reverend Bob Shuler of Trinity Methodist Episcopal Church, Aimee went swimming on May 18, 1926, and vanished in the Pacific. It was assumed she had drowned. Nobody could locate the body. Ma Kennedy maintained a vigil. The press waited, too.

Suddenly, ransom notes demanding half a million dollars reached Ma Kennedy. If Ma did not pay up, the kidnappers would "sell her [Sister Aimee] to old Felipe of Mexico City."

On the morning of June 23, Captain Herman Cline of the Los Angeles police awakened Ma Kennedy with the news that he had received word that her "drowned" daughter Aimee was safe and sound in Arizona.

Back in Los Angeles, Aimee told police she had been kidnapped back at Echo Beach, enticed into a waiting motor car and chloroformed. Then she was taken miles away in the car. Finally she escaped her kidnappers and found herself in the desert. Faint from thirst and burned by the sun, she staggered through the sand until she found a house on the Arizona landscape.

It was a sensational story, and quieted opposition to her evangelism when it was pointed out that criticism could cut two ways—as could publicity.

The rest of her life was devoted to evangelism. She died on September 27, 1944.

A clipping from a newspaper on January 1, 1963, read as follows:

Angelus Temple—the church built by evangelist Aimee Semple McPherson and her faithful flock—celebrated its 40th anniversary today with an all-day rally.

Anyone who attended the original dedication was invited to participate by the temple's pastor, Dr. Rolf K. McPherson, son of the founder.

Back in the roaring 1920's, Sister Aimee gathered crowds and headlines matching those of today's evangelist Billy Graham.

# CHAPTER THIRTEEN

# The Crusaders

When Billy Graham became a national figure in 1950, he unconsciously assumed leadership of a quickly growing evangelical movement. The movement was actually the outgrowth of a group of sophisticated theological conservatives who had joined forces in the 1940s with Carl F. H. Henry and Edward John Carnell.

This movement advocated a neo-fundamentalist faith that had grown out of a modernist-fundamentalist theological controversy that occurred in the 1920s. In addition, the neo-fundamentalists stressed the need for Christians to understand the economic, social and political currents of American life.

This group seriously challenged the "liberal" Protestant sects which had survived the two wars. In 1950 the organization of the National Council of Churches was confronted by a brand-new group called the National Association of Evangelicals, a loosely formed organization of neo-fundamentalists. In the period when Billy Graham first came to national prominence, he had a choice: He could stick with the fundamentalists, who were close to the church of his origin, or he could join the neo-evangelicals and the NAE.

Billy Graham was becoming adept at handling press conferences. The press, on its side, was waiting for the bubble to burst. News editors figured that Billy Graham was a nine-day wonder and would fade quickly once the novelty of his image and his product had worn off.

Meanwhile, the Graham team was giving a long hard look at the current state of evangelism. Upon Hay-

maker's suggestion, as indicated previously, they renamed their meetings "Crusades," substituting the new
word for "campaign" or "revival." At the same time,
they changed the old-fashioned term "personal worker"
to "counselor," a term used in education and social
work but never previously used in religion.

They made it a rule never to visit a city unless they
had been invited by a substantial group of representative churches.

They went from city to city with energy and forth-
rightness, staging four-to-five-week campaigns everywhere. They left behind hosts of friends and converts—
and occasionally some bitter critics.

Oddly enough, it was the conservative clergymen who
became their most vociferous enemies. They felt that
the Graham team was ignoring the Sacraments. Billy
was also accused of associating with men of false beliefs about the Bible, the Atonement and other "fun-
damentals of the faith."

He was urged to separate himself from all those
who were unsound. Billy felt these critics would have
condemned St. Paul for preaching in a synagogue.

What hurt him most was that conservatives whose
friendship he valued highly—men like Dr. John R. Rice
and Dr. Carl McIntire—suddenly lashed out against
him.

At the same time, however, by placing himself at the
head of the forces of the National Association of Evangelists, Billy Graham was gaining a distinct advantage.
In the next two decades, the NAE would prosper, and
the National Council of Churches would stumble after
falling into disfavor with large blocks of constituents.

A much larger group of theologians, however,
thought Billy's theology was old-fashioned. When he
heard that he had set back Christianity fifty years by
his actions, he replied:

"I am disappointed. I had hoped to put it back two
thousand years."

Ministers of the liberal persuasion which had been
so successful during the opening years of the century

were astonished and not a little puzzled by his obvious success with the masses of people.

*The Christian Century* wrote about these liberal ministers: "They agreed that Graham is sincere, but deplored his theological literalism and his appeal to fear. While holding his homiletics immature, they recognize the great strength of his preaching, attributing it to his personality, his sensationalism, his publicity techniques and his burning conviction that he is indeed a latter-day prophet."

In spite of such sniping, a widening range of church support arrayed itself behind him in the 1950s. He was pleased and gratefully accepted all good will and aid of any person in the church.

And he appreciated and used any help from men who believed in what he was doing, no matter what their theology, if they would cooperate with his platform.

In 1952 Billy Graham was the most widely heard preacher in America. As the spearhead of a new ecumenicism, he was literally breaking down barriers raised by many years of theological infighting.

He had sprung from fundamentalist beginnings, but he had widened his horizons to take in a much larger number of converts. And now it was the fundamentalist critics who wrote cold, bitter and demeaning letters and vitriolic articles. They did not seek him out to "counsel with me, pray with me, talk with me, love me."

His first instinct was to reply to them, but instead he went to the Scriptures and adopted the attitude of Nehemiah:

"I am doing a great work, so that I cannot come down: why should the work cease, whilst I leave it, and come down to you?"

When he did, infrequently, reply to criticism, it was usually in the form of what Willis Haymaker called "a love letter." No one could take offense with his words. He would take the humble place, and be just like a son to a father. He took that position because God honored it.

The year 1952 marked Billy Graham's first postwar trip to a battlefront. The Korean War was then in its third winter. For more than a year the front lines had been stabilized, and a ceasefire had come and gone.

There was fighting all along the lines. The war dead totaled more than twenty-one thousand. After a difficult and not wholly successful Pittsburgh Crusade, Billy Graham decided to spend Christmas Day with the troops.

Washington was not happy with the thought of an evangelist at the front lines; if he got killed, he might well become a martyr to peace. The Pentagon refused to approve his visit. On November 30, Jerry Beavan flew to Washington, applied some adroit pressure through friends and managed to push through Billy's request.

Eventually the necessary papers were made out for Billy and Grady Wilson. In a cliff-hanging last-minute action, the documents were delivered to the two men at the airport in Los Angeles as they waited for their flight to leave.

Washington's negative attitude to Billy's visit to the troops was totally absent in Japan and Korea. Given the temporary rank of major general, Billy Graham had at his disposal facilities and staff similar to those given Cardinal Spellman on his earlier visit.

With his team he held evangelistic services in many parts of Korea. He spent Christmas Day at the front. As he preached he could hear the sound of gunfire in the distance. He made a number of separate appearances—twice to smaller groups and once, a few miles behind, to a tremendous outdoor mass of officers and men sitting on benches or standing fully armed in the snow.

Commander in Chief Mark W. Clark commented about his visit:

"Billy Graham gave a great boost to the morale of our troops."

The visit helped Billy's ministry as well. He visited the wounded at several hospitals. Once he had to get down on the floor to look up into the face of a soldier paralyzed by bullet fragments in his spine. The man could only lie face downward.

Billy saw human suffering far beyond any previous experience.

Grady Wilson later said:

"Billy began preaching with more compassion than ever before. I could tell a big change as soon as he got back to the States. I would put it down as one of the turning points."

Upon his return from Korea, Billy Graham flew to New York, where he had been called to a conference by President-elect Dwight D. Eisenhower.

He had met the General in Paris the previous March, and again in Denver, at the time of the election campaign. During the Denver meeting Billy had presented the General with a personally inscribed Bible.

Eisenhower did not regularly attend church, he told Billy, but he did profess faith in God. He did not then belong to any specific church, nor would he join one at that time, he explained to Billy. He was afraid that it might be considered hypocritical, an outright attempt to get votes.

Billy understood his reasons for not joining then, and he appreciated the General's candor in telling him.

Now, a week before Eisenhower's inauguration, in January 1953, the two men met together in New York. In a Commodore Hotel room they talked for half an hour.

The President-elect observed at one point during the conversation that perhaps he had been successful in his election campaign because people were hoping he would set a new moral and spiritual tone in the nation. Therefore, he told Billy, "I want to introduce a spiritual and religious note in my inaugural address."

"General," Billy replied, "you can do more to inspire the American people to a more spiritual way of life than any man alive."

They discussed possible Bible passages to quote. One of those offered by Billy was Psalms 33:12, which reads:

"Blessed is the nation whose God is the Lord; and the people whom he hath chosen for his own inheritance." Another was a verse from II Chronicles. The President eventually used the verse from II Chronicles, 7:14:

"If my people, which are called by my name, shall humble themselves, and pray, and seek my face, and turn from their wicked ways; then will I hear from heaven, and will forgive their sin, and will heal their land."

In addition, Eisenhower closed his inaugural address with a prayer, the first prayer offered publicly by a President at his inauguration.

The fact that he did so was as much a surprise to Billy Graham as it was to those who heard it for the first time.

It was during Eisenhower's administration that the civil rights issue began receiving favorable attention from the federal government. Born and brought up in the South, Billy Graham had the average Southerner's typical attitudes about people. However, he had never really been comfortable with segregation.

"From the time I was converted," he once said, "I could not understand segregation in the church."

In 1952 only a few forward-looking liberals, religious leaders, and fearless black pastors were speaking out against segregation. As yet, the word "integration" had not been used as a substitute for "desegregation."

During its Crusades in the South the Graham team left the seating arrangements to the local committees. Publicly, Billy began to deplore the Jim Crow laws, and from the very first insisted that whites and blacks come forward together at the call.

"There's no racial distinction here," he said from the pulpit. "Here are white and colored alike, standing before the cross of Christ. The ground is level at the foot of the cross."

Because controversy persisted and hypocrisy continued, Billy probed the Bible for advice on race. His conclusion was that its word allowed no grounds for practicing segregation or treating one race as inferior to another. His conclusion was a clean break with the views of many evangelists, Northern and Southern.

On March 15, 1953, a year before the Supreme Court decision of May 17, 1954, Billy mounted a deliberately integrated crusade in Chattanooga, Tennessee. Blacks were to be allowed to sit anywhere. The expected happened; there were protests and predictions of trouble from friends and enemies alike.

In those days it was a daring stand for Billy to take. His team prepared for the worst. However, when the time came, nothing happened.

To the disappointment of the team, the attendance of blacks was sparse. Those who did come huddled together, a bit nervous about mingling with whites. There were no incidents. In fact, the newspapers did not even comment on the integrated seating.

In Dallas in May and June 1953, segregated seating reappeared at the Crusade there. Reluctantly Billy accepted the dictates of the Crusade committee. However, he made it plain how he felt about segregation during an incident at his hotel.

He had been taking daily massages from a black with whom he had become good friends. They met in the lobby one afternoon just before appointment time. Graham told the masseur that they would go up in the elevator together. The black pointed out that he would have to use the back stairs.

"Nonsense," said Billy. "You come with me."

The black stepped into the elevator, but the bellman intervened. Graham blew up: "Either he rides with me, or I go to the back and walk up with him. Take your choice."

The assistant manager of the hotel hurried over and assured the hotel's distinguished guest that he could take his friend with him in the elevator.

After the Supreme Court had reached its decision, Graham insisted on integrated Crusades and seating. The Nashville and New Orleans Crusades in 1954 were completely integrated, and so were all the rest held in Southern cities from that day on.

In 1953, Billy frequently and publicly stated his conviction that the Bible does not support segregation.

"Jesus Christ belongs neither to the colored nor the white races. He belongs to all races, and there are no color lines with Christ, as He repeatedly said that God looks upon the heart."

According to biographer John Pollock, privately Billy Graham thought that the church's attitude to race was lagging far behind the secular world of sports and politics and entertainment.

On October 31, 1953, he wrote his thoughts on integration in a letter to Ralph McGill, editor of the *Atlanta Constitution.*

"There must be a process of education, and faith in Christ. Christ alone can give the love in the hearts of the two races that ultimately will ease all tensions and solve all problems in this matter."

# CHAPTER FOURTEEN

# London

In a visit to London in March 1952, Billy Graham addressed Church House, Westminster. People came out in droves to hear him. The British clergy was impressed by the attendance figures.

He then discussed evangelism with eight hundred British religious leaders. As a result of these meetings, he was invited to return and run a three-month Greater London Crusade beginning March 1, 1954.

The invitation came from a private organization, the century-old Evangelical Alliance, a group of one thousand Greater London churches of all denominations, two thirds of them Church of England.

However, the group did not include the Archbishop of Canterbury, Geoffrey Fisher. Nor would the British Council of Churches endorse the Crusade unless Billy agreed to conduct a pilot campaign around the English countryside first, which he refused to do.

By all accounts, London was judged the most difficult city Billy Graham had ever faced. British church life was at a low ebb, probably lower than at any previous time in the twentieth century.

Church membership—which was then 59 percent of the U.S. population—was between 5 and 15 percent of the British population. Against 34 percent of the U.S. population, the percentage of churchgoers in England was only 10 percent.

A magazine survey found that only ten in a group of forty Royal Air Force cadets could explain how Christmas got its name. One elderly woman was quite disturbed by the survey. "They'll be dragging religion into Christmas next!" she wailed.

The prevailing church attitude in Britain was, to put it mildly, cool to "revivalism"—and even cooler to the American version of it.

During 1952 and 1953, several visiting Englishmen attended Billy Graham Crusades in the United States and returned to tell their associates in Britain that the meetings were quite successful. However, no Briton believed that such a mission could succeed as well in England as it did in the "colonies."

There was one basic problem in getting the London Crusade off the ground. In the early 1950s the British harbored a strong generalized dislike for America. And they had always had an extreme distaste for American "hot gospel" and evangelistic ballyhoo.

Their blanket dislike of all Yanks was a direct result of their close contact with them during World War II, coupled with their obvious envy of America and its wealth.

And their distaste of ballyhoo came from their dislike of hard-sell advertising and press agentry, which they associated with the American "personality."

"We thought of Aimee Semple McPherson, and the gush of Los Angeles," wrote Cecil Northcott. "We thought of religion flowing with dollars and Coca-Cola."

When the executive committee of the Greater London Crusade finally secured an auditorium for Billy Graham, it turned out to be Harringay Arena, in the bleakest part of north London. It was an enormous concrete barn seating eleven thousand, owned by the Greyhound Racing Association.

Only dog-track gamblers and circus clowns went there. "Fancy getting converted at Harringay!" one wag said with lifted eyebrows.

Even the most popular sports events left the Harringay Arena half empty. The word was that no man in Britain, no matter how famous, could ever hope to fill it for so long as two nights in a row. And Billy Graham wanted it for three months!

When the contracts were signed, the managing director of the Association promised cooperation with the

Graham team representatives. He confidentially believed that the contract would be broken in two weeks or less.

Once the pact was inked in, Billy's counselors immediately flew to England to start work with the sponsoring committee from the Evangelical Alliance.

Jerry Beavan was appointed associate crusade director under Roy Cattell, the Evangelical Alliance secretary. Beavan's job was to do the advance work. This included organizing about five thousand home prayer meetings a week to pray for the Crusade's success, and training twenty-seven hundred counselors to follow through with the men and women making the decision for Christ.

Beavan's first announcement about promotion staggered everyone within hearing distance and almost scared the pigeons away from Trafalgar Square. He said that the publicity budget would be about fifty thousand pounds—or somewhere in the neighborhood of two hundred thousand dollars.

Major General D. J. Wilson-Heffenden, who had faced the Japanese in the Burma campaign during World War II, couldn't quite face the thought of that much advertising.

"But what's it all for?" he asked.

"Pictures of Billy."

"But do we *need* them?"

Beavan smiled. "Pictures will sell his name. We have to do a big selling job to get people to come out to hear him. Words won't do it."

The general was dubious—and upset. So were the Londoners who suddenly saw poster after poster of Billy Graham blossoming out all over the city.

The poster was simplicity itself: a huge facial shot of Billy, and the words:

HEAR BILLY GRAHAM

There were thousands of them in London, everywhere the eye could see: on the sides of six hundred buses; on one hundred and fifty billboards; on three thousand units of smaller outdoor advertising; on fifteen hundred tube-station posters; and on twenty thousand bumper stickers.

The money underwriting the ad campaign came mostly from the United States, not from the British population. And it was in raising this money that the Graham team committed a major gaffe that almost undid the entire Crusade before it got started.

To stimulate contributions, Beavan and the publicity firm working with him in the U.S. dreamed up a beautiful illustrated brochure about the need for a religious revival in Britain. The book explained the objectives of the Billy Graham Crusade and outlined the methods of achieving them.

The book was priced at twelve dollars—a fantastically large sum for a book in 1953—but the pictures and the expensive paper made it worth the price.

The first copies were ready during the Dallas Crusade held in June 1953. George Wilson brought a number of them down from Minneapolis for Billy and Jerry Beavan to see. The copies were actually hand-pulled proofs. They had been only haphazardly proofread, and contained numerous typos and misspellings. There was even one misquotation of Shakespeare.

Billy and Beavan showed one to an English businessman who was visiting Dallas during the Crusade. He spotted a linguistic slip that had an unfortunate connotation. In a paragraph describing the decline of religion during and after World War II, the writer had used the word "socialism" in a way that might be interpreted as an unintended and grievous insult to the English Labour Party, which was also called the Socialist Party.

Beavan changed the word "socialism" to "secularism" and marked the copy.

George Wilson was not present when Billy, Beavan and the Englishman discussed the word change. He returned to Minneapolis with copies that had not been marked, not knowing that the text contained a ticking time bomb.

That was the state of affairs when the Grahams and the Crusade team went to New York to board the *United States* for England in February.

Billy called on Henry R. Luce in Manhattan.

"If you can get an article in the *Daily Mirror*," Luce advised him, "or one of the newspapers with mass circulation, it will probably help."

Little did Luce or Billy dream what the London press had in store for the Graham Crusade!

On the boat trip over the main thing Billy was concerned about was the tempo at which he should speak in London. One of his advisors suggested that he articulate more slowly, and that he not shout quite so loudly when he came to the dramatic parts of his sermons.

Meanwhile, in London, the British press was, in the words of *Time* magazine later, "warming up the oven to give him a good roasting."

"America occasionally tells her friends what to do," wrote the *Daily Mirror*. "Tomorrow an American arrives in Britain to tell us what to think and what to believe. God's Own Country has always run a brisk export line in evangelists. They come in all shapes and sizes. We've had kids like seven-year-old Renée Martz, who tooted a trumpet and sang in Chinese. We've had 'Little David,' the teen-age 'miracle healer.' Now we're getting Mr. Billy Graham."

"Sagittarius," a writer for the leftist journal *New Statesman and Nation,* composed a limerick:

> The mission to save Britain from the brink
> Reveals that Saints need not from Mammon
>     shrink.
>   The world's industrial Croesus
>   In partnership with Jesus
> Brings Christ to Britain labeled "Jesus Inc."

But that was mild compared to the real shocker. The first inkling of that trouble occurred one day short of docking at Southampton, when the ship's news sheet contained this startling item:

"A Labour Member of Parliament announced today that he would challenge in Commons the admission of Billy Graham to England on the grounds the American evangelist was interfering in British politics under the guise of religion."

Billy was puzzled—and extremely upset—at the notice. Immediately he got through to Jerry Beavan in London on the ship's radiotelephone.

Beavan told him what had happened. The Crusade office had sent Hannen Swaffer, a widely read columnist on the *Daily Herald,* a high-circulation left-wing newspaper, a prayer calendar prepared by the Billy Graham Evangelistic Association in Minneapolis. There, under a photograph of London taken from the promotional brochure, appeared the original caption that had been rewritten in Dallas:

"And, when the war ended, a sense of frustration and disillusionment gripped England, and what Hitler's bombs could not do, socialism with its accompanying evils shortly accomplished."

Hannen Swaffer blew his journalistic stack. Under a screaming headline—APOLOGIZE, BILLY—OR STAY AWAY!—he wrote a sizzling diatribe. Calling him a "political adventurer in disguise," he claimed that Billy Graham had "more gravely libeled us than anyone has dared to do since the war." He said the caption was an attack on the former Socialist government and the Labour Party's fourteen million loyal supporters.

Beavan immediately sent an explanation of the fiasco to the press. But it did little good. The fact that Billy knew nothing about the blooper was no excuse, either.

The rest of the print media knew a good thing when they saw it, and they were in full cry now, out for Billy's head.

Billy and George Wilson, who took the blame for the error, wired apologies to Geoffrey de Freitas, the Member of Parliament who was going to raise the question in the House of Commons.

Going to the Bible, as he always did in times of stress, Billy read and meditated. It was all there. Opposition was inevitable. But Christ would triumph. Relieved, Billy composed a note and a friendly greeting to Hannen Swaffer which he sent to the *Daily Herald*.

Before going through customs, the boat was boarded by a tugful of excited newsmen and photographers. Ignoring a film star on board, they crowded around the Grahams. Billy now realized that the "socialism" gaffe was a blessing in disguise. It had made him front-page news, even if it wasn't "nice" news. Billy was not unaware of the time-honored axiom of public relations: Write what you want about me. Just be sure you spell my name right.

The press was hostile and brassy.

"Do you think you can save Britain?" demanded one reporter.

Another turned to Ruth: "I see you still wear make-up."

Someone widened his eyes at Billy's loud hand-painted cravat. "No clerical collar," he commented snidely, "but my! what a lovely tie!"

To Ruth: "Is it true that your husband carries around his own special jug of water for baptism?"

After the newsreel cameras had finished and a television interview had been held on the side of the dock, the Grahams went into the customs shed.

There Billy opened his suitcase. As he checked the contents, the customs officer said in a low voice: "Welcome to England, and good luck, sir. We need you."

Not a moment later, a dockworker called out: "God bless you, sir. I'm praying for you."

Next day the Graham group boarded a train for London. The team crowded into Billy's compartment to pray for the Crusade.

Billy was upset about the press's opposition. Now he turned to his wife, a little grimly. "The British evangelicals consider lipstick worldly, Ruth," he told her.

She blinked and started to say something, but held back. She knew the strain he was under.

In her diary, she later wrote: "Bill stooped from being a man of God to become a meddlesome husband and ordered my lipstick off. There was a lively argument—then I wiped it off. He got so busy getting the bags together I managed to put more on without notice. Then we were at Waterloo."

At Waterloo Station it was like a city under siege. There was a surging mass of two thousand people pushing and shoving in the crowded station. There were cheers. Some sang hymns. Others waved Bibles.

"My!" exclaimed one young girl. "You'd think it was the Queen!"

One red-faced official snorted: "If these are Christians, I'll take the lions!"

It was the biggest crowd at Waterloo Station since the arrival of Mary Pickford and Douglas Fairbanks in 1924.

People crowded around the Grahams. "God bless you," someone said to Ruth. "Welcome to England."

It was a royal welcome by the real British people.

During the next few days, Billy went twice to the House of Commons—once to apologize to Geoffrey de Freitas, who cordially showed him over the chamber and wound up calling him "a sincere Christian," and once again to speak at a dinner for Members and their guests.

Billy held a press conference in a gloomy Methodist meeting hall in Westminster Abbey. Reporters came crowding in, gleefully prepared to perform on him an exercise in exquisite agony known by the British as drawing-and-quartering.

But Billy was quick on his feet.

"I am here," he explained, "because I was invited to come. I'm not here for your money. I'm not going to preach anticommunism, antisocialism, or antiliberalism. I have come to preach Christ."

He continued, pointing out that in the last five years the world had seen the greatest religious wave in history. "It has swept the U.S.," he went on. "Arthur Godfrey now talks about religion on television."

After about a thousand well-chosen words, Billy turned to George Beverly Shea, who sang his own composition, "I'd Rather Have Jesus than Anything Else."

Newsmen were enchanted.

"He seems to have the sincerity, ingenuousness, the sort of simple charm that is the greatest fun about Americans and the quality that makes us love Danny Kaye so," one woman reporter said.

Cecil Northcott found him a "modest, nice mannered, handsome man who slapped his Bible and wore his clothes in that loose easy style which goes by the name of 'well groomed.'

"He handled the press well, distinguished Cambridge from Oxford, and said that he'd just looked in to give a hand to religion over here."

March 1, the opening day of the Crusade, dawned gray and cold and bleak. It was cheerless and chilly in London. The weather got worse. Sleet fell.

President Eisenhower had promised to have Senator Stuart Symington and Senator Styles Bridges attend the opening day at Harringay. Now a phone call to the hotel informed Billy that the two senators could not come after all. The ostensible reason was a dinner engagement. Billy was not so sure. He reasoned that the American ambassador to Britain, who had washed his hands of him because of the "socialism" blooper, had told the senators to stay away.

"I had a terrible sinking feeling," Billy wrote. "I dropped immediately to my knees in prayer and committed the entire matter to the Lord."

One hour before the Harringay meeting was to start, Beavan telephoned to say that it was sleeting out and that there were around two hundred or three hundred newspapermen, television cameras, newsreel photographers and so on.

Ruth and Billy got into a cab and drove out to the arena.

When they arrived, the forecourt of Harringay Arena was empty.

"Our hearts were prepared for whatever God had planned," Billy said later.

He threw his shoulders back and took Ruth's arm, and the two of them went on inside.

# CHAPTER FIFTEEN

# World View

The Grahams need not have worried. In spite of the fact that it was sleeting and miserable, large crowds of people were streaming in toward the Greyhound stadium.

Willis Haymaker ran out excitedly to meet them.

"Well?" said Billy.

"The arena is jammed. It is full and running over. All eleven thousand seats are taken. There are at least three thousand in the street who can't get in."

Billy went down to his dressing room, and there got another pleasant surprise. Senators Symington and Bridges were standing there together, waiting.

"I thought you had been detained," Billy said.

"We just couldn't let you down, Billy," one of them said.

The other recounted their meeting with the Prime Minister, which had taken longer than expected and which had delayed them from making an earlier appearance. They were expected at a formal dinner now, Bridges said, which the American ambassador was giving for the Foreign Secretary. They would have to rush to make the dinner engagement, but they were determined to stay and help open the Crusade by speaking for Billy.

The press was out in full force. Reporters were scampering about to interview the principals for background stories, and photographers were rushing everywhere to take pictures of celebrities and notables both English and American. There was a carnival atmosphere to the proceedings.

Billy preached from a sky-blue pulpit under a mammoth cube that hung from the middle of the roof. Biblical text was printed on each of its four sides:

"Jesus said: I am the Way, the Truth and the Life."

"Many of you here tonight are like a plane in a fog which has lost contact with the airport," he said. "You are circling round and round in the monotony, confusion and drudgery of life. You can make contact with God tonight through Jesus Christ."

Because of the popping of flashbulbs and the distraction of the newsmen rushing about, Billy hesitated at the windup of his sermon, wondering if he should make the call to Jesus Christ after all.

Hugh Gough, the Bishop of Barking, one of the most influential of Billy's sponsors, was sitting beside him. He said flatly: "Go ahead."

Billy did so.

To the astonishment of the press—and Billy himself —one hundred and seventy-eight people quietly came forward. Some of them were overcome with emotion and were in tears. Many of them were young people, but they were a cross section of the public, rich and poor, young and old, university students and "spivs" (dandies), city men and factory workers, and here and there a face well known in the illustrated papers.

Billy gave them a few words of encouragement before sending them down to the counseling room.

Second-night attendance was down because of heavy snow flurries and atrocious weather. Soon afterward, the numbers began increasing. At the end of the first week the counseling room had been enlarged already to a considerable degree.

The unusual success of Billy's effort was not lost on the press.

"London's most extraordinary phenomenon at the moment is the nightly crowds drawn by Dr. Billy Graham, the evangelist at Harringay Arena," wrote Mollie Panter-Downes in a report to the *New Yorker:*

In addition to the Arena, which is jammed every night to its capacity of eleven thousand or so by Dr. Graham and his team, it contains a second stadium, where the followers of Mammon and dogflesh go to watch greyhound racing. (There are frequent close shaves when eager disciples find themselves all but in the jaws of the wrong turnstile.)

The fact that huge queues wait patiently for the Graham meeting and many people have to be turned away from them is viewed as either a startling refutation of the accusation, often levelled in the past from pulpits to half-empty churches, that this generation of British youth is godless or a sign that a large-scale religious revival is at hand.

Something strange and delightful was happening in London, too, she wrote. There was singing in the subway: "On the tube trains taking the crowds home from Harringay, the sound of young people loudly singing hymns echoes along the station platforms, to the mild surprise of the more secular passengers. No doubt about it, London has never known anything quite like it before in anybody's memory."

In the *Daily Express* William Hickey wrote about one night he spent at Harringay:

We parked the car in front of the rows of coaches that had come from the South, the West, and the North. We passed the queues and went in. They were singing hymns. The force of it hit you. I don't know quite where. But I felt different.

Billy-Graham is not a particularly good preacher. But it doesn't matter. The choir leader and his wretched trombone don't matter a tinker's cuss. What did matter was that thousands of British people were there who were feeling the need of God.

A button in the human mind had been pressed and a fantastic reaction had taken place, a reaction that made those releases of atomic energy small-time stuff.

"Shall we pray?" said Graham. Every head was bowed. Every eye closed. "I am going to ask you to come and stand quietly here, to surrender yourself to Christ."

And then the wooden boards of the hall started to creak under the footfalls. I shall never forget that creaking as long as I live. Some hurried. Some walked slowly with measured tread. The choir was singing softly, the same verse over and over again.

A man and a woman walked forward hand in hand. A man followed them in tears, his head bowed. They all went forward singing—just as they did in Nero's arenas, with a smile of unearthly happiness on their lips.

"This is God's doing," said Graham. "There is no other answer."

He never spoke more truly.

A correspondent for *The Christian Century* wrote:

What was announced as a "Greater London" crusade looks as if it might become an "All-England" crusade. The Graham organization has done an effective publicity job; at least it has compelled press and radio to take notice. The mass-circulation papers have given plenty of space to the campaign.

The build-up for the meetings—magnificent singing, trumpet solos, "audience management"—is new to Britain, and many go to see the show. . . .

In assessing the "power" of Billy Graham, Britishers note that he is not eloquent, that he is not emotional, that he uses no twist of phrase likely to hold attention. They would not place him among the "great preachers." His speaking method consists of sharp, emphatic pronouncements on fundamental Bible themes, with much repetition.

His harsh, metallic voice is unpleasant. He obviously relies on the effect of well drummed phrases passing through the minds of the "mass audience" which has been conditioned by choruses and beautifully rendered gospel solos.

Undoubtedly, many young people like to have a religious experience conveyed in this manner. This may be a religion of sorts, but serious observers ask, Is it Christian?

Further analyzing Billy's impact, Cecil Northcott wrote:

Graham has mystified British observers in his almost studied avoidance of emotion. He makes no appeal, except the subtle one of his own presence. He leaves behind in the memory no memorable phrases. As an orator he is flat and dull. Where then lies his power? Plainly he is being used as a channel of communication. There is no other explanation. There are many things that Billy Graham is not. There is one thing that he is—a man of God.

One newspaper editorialized:

Will anyone deny that this is precisely the message our generation needs? If Mr. Graham can indeed rekindle the faith that makes life worth living, then it would be wrong to doubt either the sincerity or power of his mission just because he surrounds it with the trappings of modern propaganda. . . .

Uncertainty is breeding aimlessness. It is hard in the cold caverns of fear to discover the sweetness that lies in the sun and the stars and the wind on the heath.

Billy visited Cambridge one day to address the undergraduates at the university. When he had ended his address, he left the hall after asking those who wished to make a decision for Christ to remain.

Fifteen minutes later he returned. The entire audience was still sitting there! He explained that only those who wished to make a decision should stay.

Three times he returned, thinking that there was a misunderstanding. Finally he realized that all the young men and women in the hall had chosen to stay. Then he asked them to come forward, and all rose spontaneously to make their decision.

"Truly a surprising occurrence for Cambridge!" commented *The Christian Century*.

One of the hymns sung at Harringay caught on with the public in London, and soon was heard being sung all over town. "To God Be the Glory, Great Things He Hath Done" was actually written in the nineteenth century by two Americans, Fanny Crosby and W. H. Doane. It was heard as much as the pop songs on the top-ten list.

There were conversions by the thousands at the arena. Most of them were conversions of the average man, the not-well-known, but some were of personalities known everywhere, or businessmen who were rich and respected.

For seventy-two nights—six nights a week for twelve weeks—Billy Graham filled Harringay Arena, except for four nights when there were bad storms. Sometimes two and even three evening services were needed to take care of the overflow. A hall seating twenty-five thousand could have been filled each night.

By means of leased telephone lines the Harringay services were sent to audiences in four hundred communities throughout England, Scotland and Wales. In addition, Billy spoke to millions of Britons by television and radio during his stay.

On the last day of the Crusade, sixty-five thousand people filled White City, an outdoor stadium, and on the evening of the last day, one hundred and twenty thousand filled Wembley Stadium.

In all, between 1,750,000 and 2,000,000 persons heard Billy Graham in London and there were an incredible 38,000 who made the decision for Christ. Titled nobility, Members of Parliament, businessmen, factory and shop workers and intellectuals all felt the impact of the Crusade. A number of alcoholics were converted and began attending church.

The Graham team matured considerably during the English experience. Billy began to speak more slowly and quietly, and toned down the more athletic aspects of his delivery. He gave up the loud ties which had always been a hallmark of his appearance but which gave him the look of a dandy. Cliff Barrows stopped using his trombone to whomp up the singing.

And England itself was never the same again.

In summing up, the *London Sunday Times* wrote:

Three months ago a young American came to London. His arrival was greeted in some quarters either with ridicule and hostility or with contemptuous silence. But religion has become front-page news and frequent articles have been printed either about "Billy" Graham or concerning the challenge he has brought to the Churches.

Religion is now a popular subject for conversation. Behind this there is revealed a longing in the heart of man, a sense of hunger for something he hardly knows what, a reaching out for that which can satisfy those hitherto unspoken yearnings deep within him.

Dr. Graham has appeared in the role of an Old Testament prophet or a John the Baptist declaring "Thus said the Lord God," and thousands have responded to his message.

Before it happened it would have seemed incredible that one preacher, however gifted, could, in the same day, have packed the White City and then, in the far greater area of Wembley Stadium, drawn 120,000 people together in an act of worship.

This extraordinary young man has done his part and done it magnificently. What opportunities await the Church to follow up with the same zeal the lead with which he has stirred so many hearts!

And the *Daily Telegraph* said: "When Mr. Billy Graham's visit to this country was announced it was widely feared that he was another American 'hot gospeler' after the manner of Aimee McPherson. Such impressions were quickly dispelled by his charm, sincerity, and simplicity bound together by a deep Christian charity."

Billy Graham himself had this to say about England: "We have fallen in love with the British people, and I trust that one of the byproducts of this campaign has been the betterment of Anglo-American relations."

Earlier in the crusade, Billy had written an invitation to Prime Minister Winston Churchill to come to Wembley on the last night of the crusade. Churchill said he could not. But newspaper reports of the Wembley meeting impressed him so much that he invited Billy to come to see him privately.

At noon on Monday, May 24, Billy Graham was ushered into Number 10 Downing Street. The Prime Minister explained that he had been reading about the Greater London Crusade and was happy to have the American come to England, because he thought the country needed an emphasis on Christ, and besides, he was half American himself!

Suddenly he looked directly into Billy's eyes. "Do you have any hope? What hope do you have for the world?"

Billy took out his copy of the New Testament. "Mr. Prime Minister, I am filled with hope."

According to John Pollock's biography, the Prime Minister then pointed to three London evening papers lying on a table nearby, mentioning that their news columns were filled with rape, murder and hate.

"I am an old man," Churchill said, and added, "without hope for the world."

"Life is very exciting even if there's a war," Billy said, "because I know what is going to happen in the future."

He said that was the reason he was full of hope. He told about Jesus Christ, beginning at the beginning, then skipping from place to place in the New Testament, explaining the meaning of Christ's birth, His death, His resurrection and ascension, and how a man can be born again like Jesus.

The interview, scheduled for five minutes, lasted forty. At last Sir Winston said: "I do not see much hope for the future unless it is the hope you are talking about, young man. We must have a return to God." He stood up and shook Billy's hand. "Our conversation is private, isn't it?" he asked with a smile.

Billy indicated that it was. Nor did he ever mention a word that had been said between them during Sir Winston's lifetime, except for a phrase or two. All the press learned as Billy left Number 10 Downing Street was that he thought of himself as "shaking hands with Mr. History."

It was a fitting climax to Billy Graham's first Crusade outside the United States.

Following the Greater London Crusade, the Graham team held meetings in Helsinki, Stockholm and Copenhagen, and then went on to Amsterdam, Germany and France. A Scotland Crusade followed, with a return to Britain in 1955.

The next big Crusade was scheduled for India, in January 1956. An invitation from the Evangelical Fellowship of India had been endorsed by almost every church and mission there except the Roman Catholic.

Before leaving New York for Asia, Billy told his colleagues: "As He was with me in Scotland and in England and in Germany and in France and in America, so will He be with us in India."

During the Crusade Billy met with Prime Minister Nehru. At first Nehru simply sat and listened to Billy as he talked about America, extended the greetings the President had sent through him and talked the platitudes of politics. However, when he finally dropped the "State Department" façade and began talking about the Bible, the Prime Minister became quite interested, and the two men discussed religion with animation and enthusiasm.

The tour of India was capped by one-day meetings

in Manila, Hong Kong, Formosa, Japan, Korea and Hawaii.

When Billy returned, Eisenhower discussed the Crusade at a press conference. The President said that he considered Billy Graham a man who clearly understood that man is, after all, a spiritual being. That fact had to be understood by the world before any advance in man's condition could be made.

And he pointed out that the evangelist was exceptional because he carried his convictions to the far corners of the earth, where he used his religious concepts trying to promote mediation instead of conflict and tolerance instead of prejudice.

# CHAPTER SIXTEEN

# Home

In 1955 the Grahams invested their savings to buy a two-hundred-acre piece of mountaintop land above the town of Montreat in Black Mountain. The woodland, costing twelve dollars an acre, was completely undeveloped.

There they began to build a new home, financed in part from a building fund begun by ten business friends at Montreat and elsewhere.

Since 1946 they had lived in a comfortable but very modest cottage on Assembly Drive, one of the main roads into the Montreat conference grounds. From 1949 on, the house had become something of a tourist landmark as the name of Billy Graham spread far beyond the confines of North Carolina.

Located behind a thin screen of shrubs, the tiny cottage was vulnerable and accessible to all. Billy Graham fans would wander inside the grounds, tear down pieces of shubbery for souvenirs, and peer into the windows in typical rubberneck fashion.

They began taking snapshots not only of the house but of the children. Soon sightseeing buses included the Graham house in their itinerary. There was no privacy to be had. Some of the more brash tourists even gave the children dimes to pose for pictures, until Ruth put a stop to it.

It was during Billy's Crusade in India that Ruth came home to supervise the construction of a new house on the mountainside plot. And it was her own inventiveness that gave it its distinctive old-fashioned flavor.

She began scouring the mountains nearby, buying old lumber from abandoned cabins and purchasing second-hand brick from a schoolhouse that had been torn down. She got materials of all kinds from both likely and unlikely sources.

What she wanted was a house that fitted into the mountainside environment. The aged and weathered lumber and masonry she acquired was just right. When the house was finally built, it looked a hundred years old, and it blended in beautifully with the rustic, rugged terrain around it.

The interior she made into an informal country home atmosphere, just like the kind that her grandparents had probably lived in during the nineteenth century.

"I want it to be a home that everyone can feel at home in, whether mountainfolk or the wealthy," she once told Billy. It became exactly that.

In the back yard, a huge excavation was scooped out of the mountainside. A running brook was then dammed up to make a swimming pool for the children.

The main advantage of the house was its location. It could be reached only by a winding, one-way road too narrow and twisting for buses to negotiate and built strictly for the most daring of drivers.

The idea behind the solitude was to provide a place to which Billy Graham could return at the end of a Crusade to "recharge his batteries," looking out over the superb view and breathing the pure North Carolina mountain air. Solitude and quiet for her husband were to be the keynotes of the house.

Billy's study, designed by a Greensboro friend and prefabricated and shipped to Montreat for on-site assembly, was placed so that it was isolated from the rest of the house and provided a perfect work area.

By 1955 there were five Graham children. The family was complete. Although Ruth had said once she wanted six, the Grahams decided that three girls and two boys was a good-sized family, large enough to provide balance and the proper environment for growing up.

The oldest, Virginia Leftwich, was born on September 21, 1945, two years after the Grahams were married. She was nicknamed Gigi.

Next came Anne Morrow, born in 1948. The third girl was Ruth Bell, born in December 1950.

In July 1952, the first son, William Franklin, was born, followed by Nelson Edman, called Ned, in 1955.

Gigi was the first to marry. It was one of her father's books that brought her in contact with her husband-to-be.

Stephan Tchividjian was born and brought up in Switzerland, where he lived with his family. The family maid had been converted to Christianity, and had left one of Billy Graham's books on a bedside table. Stephan's father read it and became converted himself. The whole family followed.

In 1957 the Tchividjians visited the United States, where Billy Graham was conducting a mammoth New York Crusade at Madison Square Garden. The Swiss family met the evangelist, and the entire Graham family was invited to visit the Tchividjians in Switzerland in 1960. That was where Gigi met Stephan. Gigi was only fifteen at the time. Two years later Stephan wrote a letter to her, proposing.

As she drove to the airport to meet him, she prayed all the way to be enlightened by God as to whether this was the man for her. She found her answer. "This is of God, Daddy," she later told her father.

They were married in 1962.

Stephan Tchividjian and his wife moved to Jacksonville, Florida, where Stephan began studying to be a psychologist. The couple have four children: Basil, Bridgette, Stephan and Tulian.

Anne Morrow met her future husband, Daniel Lotz, at a conference of Christian Athletes one summer. Soon they fell in love. They were married shortly afterward, and the Lotzes moved to Raleigh, North Carolina, where Danny practices dentistry. They have two children.

"Bunny"—Ruth Bell—met her husband in 1966 on one of her father's Crusades in London. He was Ted

Dienert, son of Fred Dienert, a partner in the advertising agency that started Billy Graham out in radio on *Hour of Decision,* and that now handles most of the Billy Graham Evangelistic Association's work.

The couple moved to Valley Forge, Pennsylvania, to live. Ted is an advertising executive. Bunny herself is an active evangelist, handling several Bible classes and speaking frequently.

William Franklin attended college at Montreat Anderson, and Ned, the youngest, attended a boarding school in England before returning to the United States for further education.

Although none of the daughters finished college, a fact which didn't sit too well with their college-educated parents, they were married to men fully approved of by the Grahams.

Speaking for all the children, Bunny Graham Dienert recently wrote: "You can say that all of us children have chosen to live the way Daddy and Mother wanted us to, with each day a new commitment to Jesus, and a new dedication of our lives to Him. But there's really nothing special about that."

During the years that they were growing up, Ruth Graham tried to raise a family that would be normal and happy, a family capable of making each individual a rounded and happy person.

In her household chores, Ruth Graham had the full-time assistance of Beatrice Long, a daily maid, and John Rickman, who acted as caretaker of the two-hundred-acre holding.

The house always had its share of animals as well as children. In fact, Ruth used to refer to it as a Noah's ark of "happy confusion." The menagerie consisted at various times of a Great Dane, a huge white Pyrenees dog named Belshazzar, puppies, cats, pet birds, a Suffolk ram, three Hampshire sheep and even a mule.

Billy was enthusiastic about the acquisition of the sheep. "They can keep down the grass," he told Ruth, "and we've got to have sheep and goats and things like that so the kids will learn the facts of life."

Ruth sighed at the thought. "Billy, why don't I just tell them and save us all that trouble?"

She might better have. In his exuberance at being a gentleman farmer on a mountaintop, Billy was one day feeding his flock of animals a basket of apples. The ram, an aggressive beast, took solid aim and butted Billy over the side of the rocky cliff. He got a hairline fracture in his left tibia—very painful—torn ligaments of the left knee, and cuts, bruises and contusions all over.

Everybody thought it was a very funny thing, a man of God being delivered over a cliff by a satanic creature with cloven hoofs. Billy was not amused.

Billy's love of animals was all part of his character. Ruth wrote once that she had seen him in a very deep spiritual conversation with a visitor while kittens played around his legs.

When he was ill once after a Crusade she went in to find one of the huge dogs lying beside him on the bed. A Saint Bernard named Heidi used to watch television shows with him, her head moving from side to side as she followed all the action on the screen.

Ruth Graham once had this to say about homemaking: "To me, it's the nicest, most rewarding job in the world, second in importance to none, not even preaching. In fact, maybe it is preaching."

She used to join Billy on many of his Crusades, but during the crucial times when the children were growing up, she stayed home. "A mother, like the Lord, needs to be a very present help in times of trouble. A mother has to be with the children. Personally, I love it."

But she continued to miss her husband because he was away so much of the time traveling.

"Personally, I wish we could be more normal. But God never asks us to give up one thing without giving so much in return that you wind up almost ashamed of yourself."

Asked once if she ever spanked her children as they were growing up, she laughed and replied: "Do I spank my children? Heavens yes! I cope with home repairs, too. Billy can't drive a nail."

She summed it up one time by writing: "Although we don't have a normal family life, we have a happy one."

Discipline was firm, with the rules carefully spelled out. If they were broken, punishment was swift. It was generally in the form of a shoe tree applied to the offender's bottom by Ruth Graham.

During the early days of their life together, with Billy away a great deal of the time, Ruth was forced to do most of the chores around the house. She had to repair appliances when she could, feed the livestock when necessary, and she drove their topless jeep on mountain roads to run errands and to gather white oak logs for the fireplace.

While she did the housework, she carried the Bible around with her. In fact, she made it a practice to read a chapter of Proverbs every day. She would become so absorbed in the Bible that she would miss a bed here and there and forget to sweep certain parts of the floor.

"There is always something new and wonderful to find in the Bible," she told an interviewer. "Since I don't really enjoy housework anyway, it lightens the load."

The Grahams have never smoked, played cards, danced or gone to the theater. In spite of that, there has always been a touch of worldliness in Ruth that kept the piety in her from turning into treacle.

She has always been able to bring Billy Graham down to earth when he needs it, too. She has an unawed attitude about him that guards him against pontification and—most important of all—the sin of pride.

One time when they were first married and very short of funds, Billy carelessly put what he thought was a dollar bill in the collection plate and then, when it was too late, saw to his consternation that it was a ten-dollar bill.

He reached out to take it back, but Ruth stopped him.

"There's nothing you can do about it," she told

him. "And in the eyes of the Lord," she said, rubbing it in, "you'll not get credit for ten dollars either, since one dollar was all you planned to give."

At another time, when he had finished preaching a sermon he particularly liked, he asked her what she thought of it.

"It was a good sermon except for the timing," she told him.

Billy was puzzled. "What do you mean, the timing?"

"You spent eleven minutes on a wife's duty to her husband and only seven on a husband's duty to his wife," she informed him acidly.

She has been quoted as saying that life as a preacher's wife is quite different from what the general public thinks:

"Life in the Graham household is not a matter of uninterrupted sweetness and light. Nor is it a matter of uninterrupted agreement.

"At the beginning of our marriage some very wise person told me that when two people agree on everything, one of them is unnecessary.

"But you've got to keep your sense of humor handy when you disagree. If you do, if you don't take things too seriously, then disagreeing can even be a lot of fun."

During the period when Billy was away on the first of the big Crusades, Ruth's main job was to try to put ten to twenty pounds back on her husband's frame after he returned. She has never been what would be called a superb cook, but she has always known how to make good Chinese dishes, many of them learned in China when she was a child. With the help and training of a marvelous cook who used to work for her parents in Montreat, Ruth has learned how to cook Southern-style food.

She began to give Billy what he had always had as a child: country ham, steak, potatoes, and hot biscuits with sorghum molasses. As for Billy Graham, like many non-gourmet Americans, he could be happy each meal of his life with a good steak.

Ruth Graham handled the finances that ran the house, too. It was not always easy to meet a tight budget. The children needed food and clothing—some of which Ruth made herself—and expenses were high.

The girls would wash windows and pick up pine-cones for their fifty-cent-a-week allowance. There was certainly no abundance of money flowing in.

Occasionally money would be sent to the Graham home by well-wishers from the outside. But Billy, worried about the taint of money loosely handled, always insisted that these sums be set aside. Ruth began putting it in what was called a "help fund." Periodically the money was sent to charities or used to make Christmas baskets.

She was quite tolerant of her husband's lack of interest in managing the household.

"Billy is always in motion," she said once. "As soon as he's home he's out on the road out bear hunting in the Smokies or somewhere. But that becomes a bore when the bear doesn't show up. So he goes fishing. But he can't stand to sit on the bank and wait for a nibble.

"Then he runs home and gets on the phone, planning another Crusade, calling meetings, getting out reports, and so on. Then, in the middle of all that, he hops in the car and heads for a golf course."

An inveterate golfer, he plays whenever and wherever he can. He never really learned to concentrate well enough to be a great player, experts have reported. He would always be thinking about a sermon idea or planning a new Crusade.

Ruth Graham is a personable woman, with laughter that is quick and gay. She has a photogenic face, with the high-cheekbone structure of a typical motion picture actress. Her figure is trim and slender.

She has always worn lipstick, even though many evangelists frown on cosmetics. She prefers to walk in flat sandals. When she shops, she wears bright full-flowing skirts and loose blouses.

Many of these are clothes she makes herself. And

she spent many hours making clothes for her children when they were growing up.

Her clothes are smart, whether made by herself or purchased. Because she is a female counterpart to Billy Graham—who wears nicely tailored and stylish clothes—she is a happy subject for a news photographer or television cameraman.

She dresses like a conservatively attired affluent woman. One newsman was surprised to find her so pretty. "She is not quite," he said, "but *almost* beautiful." Dressing well is part of her background and training.

When she was in England during the Greater London Crusade, she helped with the counseling in the Inquiry Room, where converts met after answering the call.

One of Ruth's converts turned out to be Joan Winmill, a well-known English actress.

"I didn't know then that she was Mrs. Billy Graham," the actress later said. "But the first thought that came to my mind when I saw her was: how much sooner people like me might have been attracted to Christianity if we had met a few such attractive Christians."

In explanation, Ruth said, "We were brought up on the mission field. But mother always hoped we wouldn't look like the pickings from a missionary barrel. Thanks to her magic touch, I don't think we ever did.

"It doesn't seem to me to be a credit to Christ to be drab. I think it's a Christian's duty to look as nice as possible. Besides, not caring about one's appearance goes against a woman's nature. That's not going to make anybody a better Christian, either. And it's not fair to the people who have to look at you."

How good-looking and attractive Ruth Graham can be was illustrated by an episode that occurred in London during the Greater London Crusade.

One Sunday afternoon just after lunch, when her husband had gone on to a meeting, Ruth went out for a walk from the hotel and headed for Hyde Park Corner. There was a big crowd there, and as she walked from one group to another she listened to the speakers expounding on their political and social views.

Suddenly it started to rain. Ruth had left her umbrella back at the hotel, and she started to run for shelter. As she proceeded on toward the hotel, she realized that someone from the crowd had fallen in beside her—a nice-looking young man, smoking a cigarette.

"Pardon me," he said politely. "Where are you going?"

"Back to my hotel," Ruth responded, thinking that in spite of the young man's politeness, he was being pushy.

"An American?" the man asked.

"That's right," said Ruth. The two of them were by that time crossing the busy street and dodging traffic. Big drops of rain were coming down harder.

"Have time for a cup of coffee?" he asked her with a smile.

"No thanks. I'd better get back."

"How about tomorrow night? Are you busy?"

"Yes," Ruth replied. "I'm going out to Harringay." Then Ruth turned to the man. "Couldn't you come?"

His eyes lighted up. "Perhaps I could. How about Tuesday night?"

"I'll be going out to Harringay Tuesday night, too." Ruth was beginning to enjoy herself by that time, as she wrote later.

"Tuesday night too!" The young man was incredulous. "Well, will you be going to Harringay every night this week?"

"Every night," Ruth assured him.

The young man blinked. "You wouldn't be connected with Billy Graham, would you?"

"His wife," Ruth replied, and burst out laughing. "But I do hope you will come." She turned down Oxford Street in the rain.

"I might," he muttered, and vanished.

She never saw him again. The joke was on him. But it was quite a tribute to her attractiveness that she could be almost picked up by a London sharpy.

Ruth can be quite amused when the joke is on her, as well. Not long after the Hyde Park incident, Ruth was chatting with the Bishop of Worcester. Somehow the name of D. L. Moody, the famous American evangelist who had spent some time in England, came up.

"I was wondering if you had ever attended any of Mr. Moody's meetings?" Ruth said offhandedly.

The Bishop looked at her strangely, and said only, "No. I was not *quite* old enough."

Billy had to tell his wife what she should have known long before:

"Moody preached in London eighty years ago, Ruth."

"No wonder the Bishop looked at me so funny!" Ruth gasped and started to giggle.

An interviewer once asked Ruth what part of her life she was most thankful for.

"I would say that I am most grateful for the hard places. You know, that's when the Bible comes to life for me. It's when the presence of the Lord is most real.

"It's not true that Billy and I have had no major problems with our children. But I could not tell you about them personally. Each crisis has taught us so much of God and also of compassion and understanding for other parents."

About prayer, Ruth has said that she has felt its efficacy many times.

"At two A.M. once I was reading the Bible, praying through a difficult situation—I forget exactly what it was now. But while I prayed, I could feel an overwhelming sense of the very presence, the very immensity of God.

"I felt a sudden flood of reassurance. And I knew once again that He is quite capable of handling our situations—all our human troubles. In His own time and in His own way. We should take care of the possible, and leave the impossible up to God."

# CHAPTER SEVENTEEN

# New York and Australia

When he left London in 1954, Billy Graham had told his team: "I have never had the faith to tackle New York, Chicago, or Philadelphia, but if God can accomplish this in London, He can accomplish it in other cities."

New York was particularly scary. It had a complex mixed population, it had Wall Street, it had Madison Avenue, it had the biggest population in the United States, it had the publishing business, the clothing business, and it was absolutely involved totally in the production of the things which made America materialistic and affluent.

It was a challenge that was frightening and at the same time irresistible.

In a Protestant country, New York Protestants were in a minority to Roman Catholics and Jews, and churchgoing in Manhattan was at an all-time low because of the cynicism and secularity of the postwar years.

According to Jesse Bader, head of Evangelism for the National Council of Churches, "To do evangelistic work in New York is like digging in flint."

Yet an invitation came from the Protestant Council of the City of New York, representing seventeen hundred churches of thirty-one denominations, and from a group of independent bodies.

Finally Billy decided to make the run for New York. The Crusade was scheduled to begin on May 15, 1957, in Madison Square Garden.

Immediately the theological press began its attacks.

*The Christian Century* sneered at the move as a "trumped-up revival" that would "spin along to its own kind of triumph because of canny, experienced engineers of decision who have laid the tracks, contracted for the passengers, and will now direct the traffic which arrives on schedule. The Graham procedure does its mechanical best to 'succeed' whether or not the Holy Spirit is in attendance. At this strange new junction of Madison Avenue and Bible Belt, the Holy Spirit is not overworked; He is overlooked."

The conservatives were in full cry, too. They hit at him for being sponsored by "modernists," even though the Crusade was sponsored not by modernists at all but by a committee of fifteen men who shared the evangelist's primarily fundamentalist aims.

Bob Jones, Sr., posted a notice that no students of Bob Jones College would be allowed to hold a prayer meeting to ask help for Billy Graham in New York. Jones claimed that it would be a repudiation of the purpose for which the university was founded. A young supporter of Billy Graham was expelled from the school, ostensibly for minor infraction of rules but actually, Billy believed, for standing up for the New York Crusade.

The Crusade opened up on schedule, and from the start broke all records for attendance, for decisions, and for total impact on the city.

"We have not come to put on a show or an entertainment," Billy Graham said on opening night to the multitudes at Madison Square Garden. "We believe that there are many people here tonight that have hungry hearts—all your life you've been searching for peace and joy, happiness, forgiveness.

"I want to tell you, before you leave Madison Square Garden this night, you can find everything that you have been searching for, in Christ. He can bring that inward deepest peace to your soul. He can forgive every sin you've ever committed. And He can give you the assurance that you're ready to meet your God, if you will surrender your will and your heart to Him.

"I want you to listen tonight not only with your ears, but the Bible teaches that your heart also has ears. Listen with your soul tonight. Forget that there's anyone else here. Forget me as the speaker, listen only to the message that God would have you to retain from what is to be said tonight.

"Shall we pray: Our Father and our God, in Christ's name we commit the next few moments to Thee, and we pray that the speaker shall hide behind the Cross until the people shall see none, save Jesus.

"And we pray that many tonight will re-evaluate their relationship to God, others will consider, for the first time perhaps, their need of God, and that many shall respond and surrender themselves to Him as they did two thousand years ago on the shores of Galilee: for we ask it in His name. Amen."

Because the Crusade was a success, it behooved the critics to evaluate the campaign in the sight of God and heaven itself.

*The Christian Century* called the message of the Crusade "A violation of the wholeness of the Christian faith." Most of the crowd, the publication claimed, were Christians anyway, and their decisions were invalid because they were not "preceded or succeeded by action of the church."

Theologian Reinhold Niebuhr wrote in *Life* magazine that Billy Graham was promising "a new life" to his converts, "not through painful religious experience but merely by signing a decision card." Niebuhr also complained that Billy Graham's evangelism failed to "explore the social dimensions of the Gospel." As a liberal, the theologian admitted that Billy had "sound personal views on racial segregation and other social issues of our time," but he claimed that "he almost ignores them in his actual preaching."

George W. Cornell, religious writer for Associated Press, disagreed, and wrote a letter to Billy Graham later.

"I have read," he stated, "various criticism of you from those who say you do not stress the full social implications of Christ's demands (the horizontal aspects, as you put it), but I have concluded that the critics simply have not paused to listen to you, but have been so dazzled by your external successes that they don't see its roots."

Dan Potter, director of the Protestant Council, said: "Billy Graham's preaching has more social content than that of the average New York minister. He says things that no minister in Manhattan dares say."

And Dr. John A. Mackay, president of Princeton Theological Seminary, wrote, "It is unfair to demand that Billy Graham should have offered a blueprint for the solution of complicated social issues in our highly industrialized mass society."

Because New York was the center of show business, the Crusade formed the Christian Actors' Fellowship, with Jerome Hines of the Metropolitan Opera Company as president and about two hundred actors and singers and stage personalities as members.

Ethel Waters, the famed black singer, actress and stage star, appeared on a television talk show. She was asked by her cynical and worldly host if she thought the crusade would fail.

Her retort made headlines:

"God don't sponsor no flops!"

After the first week in Madison Square Garden, she joined the choir of fifteen hundred voices and sang at each service for eight weeks. When Cliff Barrows learned she was there, he persuaded her to sing a solo one night.

She sang the song that she had made a hit on the stage: "His Eye Is On the Sparrow."

She told it later in her own words:

"This time, it was to be very different. The glitter and the heartache of the stage had disappeared. There was just myself, standing before eighteen thousand people, saying 'I love Jesus, too,' the only way I could say it—by singing 'His Eye Is On the Sparrow.'"

Later she appeared in a feature film based on the New York crusade, *The Heart Is a Rebel,* and went to

Crusades at her own expense to sing for the Graham team.

Seventeen of the Madison Square Garden Saturday meetings were telecast on the American Broadcasting Company nationwide. After the first telecast, over twenty-five thousand letters came in from all over the country. More than half a million letters were sent within the following three months.

In all, the New York Crusade chalked up an attendance of 2,357,400, the highest any event at Madison Square Garden had ever reached in the Garden's history. The number of decisions, in addition to those made by telecast viewers, was 61,148. Telecast viewers made some 30,000, incidentally, although some listeners obviously made the decisions without writing to tell about them.

For the closing rally, the team booked Yankee Stadium, and more than one hundred thousand attended —the largest crowd in the stadium's history.

While statistics prove physical facts, the Crusade brought a great deal more than simply a number of people to a certain place to listen to Billy Graham.

One New York minister wrote: "The real results of the crusade are not in statistical form or in ways that can be measured. You cannot tell what the crusade did for the morale of us ministers, the new confidence it gave us, the motivation it supplies for the preaching of the Bible and Christ crucified."

Billy was terribly weary after preaching ten weeks nightly without a break. Toward the end of the Crusade he would spend each day in bed, and when he spoke at night he would support himself by leaning with all his weight on the pulpit.

After the Yankee Stadium rally, the crusade was extended to sixteen weeks, and the final meeting was held in Times Square on September 1, when 1,601,000 people came to see the end of the campaign. The crossroads of the world became, in the words of the *New York Times,* "a great cathedral." The crowds spilled over into cross streets, singing hymns and listening to the words over the loudspeakers.

"Let us tonight make this a time of rededication," Billy Graham said. He began once again to preach Christ, "Who died for our sins and paid the supreme sacrifice that we might have life."

The cost of the camp Crusade, including television, came to two and a half million dollars. However, there was a surplus left for the New York committee to use. But Billy Graham was terribly exhausted after it was all over. "Something went out of me during New York that I seemingly cannot recover," he said later.

In the four months between February and May 1959, what became known as the Southern Cross Crusade was held. Invitations came from each of the six Australian states and from New Zealand. The original plan was for five weeks in Sydney, a week in Brisbane, and another in Melbourne. But Melbourne became a full-length Crusade, with two parts, as well as Sydney with a full-length crusade by Billy Graham. And shorter Crusades were formed with associate evangelists to other Australian state capitals and in three New Zealand cities.

Australia in 1959 was not opposed to Christianity, but it was definitely disinterested. It was a young nation which had grown quickly and achieved prosperity, but had never had a revival of faith. It was virgin soil for the Gospel, according to Stuart Barton Babbige and Ian Siggins in *Light Beneath the Cross,* a story about the Australia and New Zealand Crusade.

It was, they wrote, merely happily pagan, carelessly indifferent, spiritually dead.

The impact of the crusade in Melbourne, which was first on the schedule, was written by a reporter on the *Melbourne Sun* named Pat Tennison:

> Billy Graham touched down at Essendon yesterday with faith, hope, and charity ready to battle Melbourne's sin.
> As well, he showed a quick wit, sense of humor,

smooth tongue, immense patience, and wide knowledge of quotable quotes.

With it all went a ruggedly boyish face, quick toothful smile, big build, and tousled brown curly hair.

He used his many talents freely to push through the 600 hymn-singing people who greeted him; handshake the score or so of welcoming local dignitaries; then tackle almost a two-hour press conference with reporters, photographers, radio men, magazine men, and TV interviewers and cameramen.

"One of the most difficult things I have to face is the loss of personal privacy," he said, when a reporter asked if he ever became fed up with it all.

"I never did seek publicity, and how it all came about I truthfully don't know. I'd much rather be the minister of a small parish somewhere; but my wife and I decided a few years ago that as it was this way, we'd go ahead with it."

The friendly grin was frequent, but there wasn't much humor. They were pretty grim questions.

From the blunt "How is your crusade being financed?" and "Do you ever intend going to Russia?" they ranged to the subtler "Do you think some evangelists are phonies?" and "As you once studied anthropology, do you believe in evolution?"

Each he answered promptly and squarely, his voice strong and clear as any church bell, his hands cutting the air sharply, but not wildly, to emphasize points.

It was the smallest, but toughest, audience for his crusade in Australia—press conference people are just like that—and he worked hard on them.

Maybe that's why, when someone asked him what was the most prevalent and worst sin today, he smartly shot it back in one word, "Unbelief," and left a weighty pause before he went on to elaborate.

Throughout he balked only once on a question. Mentioning that he liked to relax occasionally at tennis or golf, a reporter asked his golf handicap.

"That's one of the private things I've kept private,"

he chuckled. Then he relented. "It's about 16."
Everyone was happy again.

When he left the conference room, more than 100
welcomers were still waiting to cheer him on to his
hotel.

He left not knowing that he had set at least two
airport records—the longest press conference and
one of the few at which every question was answered.

That press conference wound up with a particularly
interesting exchange.

"Are you looking for converts?" one reporter asked.

"Yes, certainly," said Billy unhesitatingly.

"Australians don't like the suggestion that they
should be converted—it's old-fashioned."

Billy answered, "On the contrary, the word 'converted' is quite a contemporary word. I have been in
fact converted during my trip to your land during the
last two or three days. I traveled by Qantas, I liked its
comfort, its competence, and the friendly service. If I
ever come this way again, I'll use Qantas. I have been
converted to Qantas." He paused. "Conversion is simply
a question of finding the right line and going with it."

Even the cops covering the conference laughed at
that one.

The press loved him. They ran pictures of the meetings every day.

Because Australia was a young continent and a young
nation, the Crusade ultimately concentrated on youth.
The most telling encounters were with university students and professors. Directly after a meeting at Melbourne University, for example, dissenters argued with
Billy for hours.

He challenged a ringleader to read the New Testament five times. Then he said, "I will pray for you, and
I predict that in ten years time you will be one of the
leaders of the Christian community in this city."

That won headlines and got good coverage. The
students wrote a letter to *Nation*, a controversial
periodical, making it clear the students felt they had

won the encounter. Within a month of their letter, two of the group were engaged in earnest conversation about the Gospel of Christ with Christian undergraduates.

*Farrago,* the University of Melbourne's weekly, published a brilliant spoof: "The Gentleman Bush Ranger, Or The Unimpressive William Graham."

"The truth of it was," the report said, "that without the celestial massed choirs, trained spotlights, fervent prayers, and booming hymns of his usual arena his emotion, sincere though it may have been, largely failed to communicate itself and his argument thus showed itself as unconnected."

Oddly enough, months later religion was still the most extensively reported topic of discussion in the columns of the university weekly. In the office of the paper the staff hung a twenty-by-thirty-inch photograph of Billy with a banner below: BIG BROTHER IS WATCHING YOU!

At Sydney University, pranksters waited until Billy had got through his presentation of the need for the Gospel of Christ. Then, suddenly, clouds of smoke poured out of a smoke bomb, and a "devil," in red cloak, horns, and tail materialized before the amused audience.

Billy was equal to the occasion. "That's my old friend the devil," he called out, ostentatiously shielding his heart with his copy of the New Testament. That reminded him of home in North Carolina.

"In a little church in our part of the world," he told the Australians, "the local boys decided they would disrupt the service. They all dressed in red, took pitchforks and rushed into the little congregation with bloodcurdling screams.

"The people got up and ran for their lives, except one sweet old lady sitting in the front pew. The ringleader rushed up to her, held out his pitchfork, and said, 'Aren't you afraid of me?' She said, 'No, Mr. Devil, I'm not afraid of you. I've been on your side for years.'"

In the three and a half months of the Southern Cross Crusade, nearly 3,250,000 people attended its meetings, equivalent to a quarter of the total Australian population. About 150,000 responded to the call.

In Billy Graham's final words of the campaign, he said:

"I hope that you will remember us in one sense, but in another sense I hope you will not remember us. I want you to remember only Christ. We came here only as His ambassadors and His messengers: to tell you that He is the Lamb of God that taketh away the sins of the world."

# CHAPTER EIGHTEEN

# Politics

During the Presidency of Lyndon B. Johnson, Billy Graham and his wife were invited to dine with the President and Mrs. Johnson. During the course of the meal the President asked Billy's opinion on a certain contemporary political problem that was bothering Johnson.

Billy opened his mouth to speak. His wife suddenly gave him a sharp kick in the ankle under the table. He shot her a pained glance, and then started to speak.

Again she kicked him.

That was too much. "Ruth," he said, "why are you kicking me?"

"Because it's none of your business, Bill."

Billy nodded. "That's just what I was going to say."

Later on, after dinner, the President came over to Ruth. "You were right, Ruth. I shouldn't have asked your husband that question."

Billy Graham's relationships with Presidents began with President Truman, who was in the White House at the time of the Los Angeles Crusade, when Billy was catapulted to national prominence. Truman's anger over Billy Graham's inadvertent revelation of the fact that the President and the evangelist had prayed together quickly brought an end to that relationship.

Eisenhower and Billy saw each other more often. It was during Eisenhower's Presidency that Billy had been involved in a great deal of international travel, taking the Gospel to other countries and continents.

In 1960, when Billy returned from the Southern

Hemisphere after conducting the successful Australia–
New Zealand Crusade, it was time for another Presi-
dential election. The two principal candidates were
Senator John F. Kennedy and Vice-President Richard
M. Nixon.

Billy had met Nixon in 1950, when he and Senator
Clyde Hoey of North Carolina were lunching in the
Senate Dining Room. As they dined, the senator from
California walked by. Nixon was invited to join them,
and Billy revealed that he had met Nixon's parents in
1948, when he was preaching at a Youth for Christ
rally in Whittier, California. Billy remembered them
because they had attended each nightly session he gave.
The Nixons were Quakers, but of an evangelical persuasion.

Nixon asked Billy to come over to Burning Tree
Country Club for a round of golf that afternoon, and
Billy—who had never been known to turn down a
golf engagement—did so. The two of them became
friends, and he would often visit the senator when he
was in Washington.

In 1960, when Nixon was the Republican nominee
for President, Billy suddenly came under heavy pressure—not from Nixon—to support the Republican
candidate. The idea was that in supporting a Republican, Billy would be tacitly repudiating the candidacy
of John F. Kennedy, a Roman Catholic. Billy was and
had always been a Democrat. Nixon was a personal
friend. Even so, his support of Nixon could be interpreted in many different ways.

Many respected Protestant church leaders were stam-
peded into the fight against Kennedy. Evangelical
leaders joined by Norman Vincent Peale met to discuss
whether a Roman Catholic President could be free of
ties to the Vatican. Billy Graham, scheduled at first to
attend the meeting, did not appear.

During the summer and autumn of 1960, he spent
most of his time engaged in Crusades in Europe. (An
amusing piece of byplay during the 1960 Crusade in
Germany was the vitriol hurled at Billy Graham by

the Communist East German press. The Communist newspapers charged that Billy Graham frequented night-clubs, and added that he was accompanied not by his wife Ruth Graham, but by a "blonde called Beverly Shea!") Before Billy left for Europe, Nixon met with him and told the evangelist that he believed it would be best if Billy did not come out for him publicly. "Your ministry," the candidate said, "is more important than my getting elected President."

On August 10 Billy wrote a letter marked "Confidential" to John F. Kennedy, denying a rumor that he would raise the religious issue in the campaign. He told Kennedy he would vote for Nixon for several reasons, including personal friendship.

Later, after Billy's return from Europe, Henry R. Luce persuaded Billy to do a magazine article for *Life* listing Nixon's merits without being partisan or revealing how he intended to vote.

Billy wrote the piece, sent it in and then had misgivings. He phoned Luce to pull the article. Luce was reluctant to. Billy and Ruth prayed:

"Oh God, if it is not Your will for this article to go—stop it!"

Meanwhile, Kennedy heard about the proposed article and called up Luce to protest. Kennedy proposed that the magazine run two parallel pieces—one about Kennedy and the other about Nixon, with a prominent Protestant clergyman doing the Kennedy piece.

Luce demurred, called Billy and told him he had decided against the article.

Billy wrote another piece called "Why Every Christian Should Vote." Luce thought it weak, but ran it anyway in the November 7 issue.

After being elected, Kennedy invited Billy to meet him in Florida for a round of golf. On the night before the game, however, Kennedy's son, John, was born, and the meeting was postponed. Five days after Kennedy's inauguration, Billy came to the White House for an exchange of ideas. They had later meetings, in which religious matters were constantly among the subjects discussed. They enjoyed a "developing friendship," according to biographer John Pollock.

A member of Kennedy's White House staff had another opinion, however. Kennedy did see Billy, but "gritted his teeth sometimes," the aide said.

Admittedly, Billy had reservations about Kennedy's Catholicism. "Subconsciously," he said once, "I am sure I had some questions as to what influence the Vatican might have over a Catholic President. But the reason I voted for Mr. Nixon—and I wrote John Kennedy this—was that I felt he was the best-trained, the best man, and because I had known him for years."

Later Kennedy and the evangelist held a press conference at the Towers Hotel, where they stood side by side and exchanged compliments.

Billy said later that Kennedy's election would help relations between Protestant and Catholic churches. "I think also that his election proved that there was not as much religious prejudice in the United States as many people feared."

During the Kennedy years Graham visited with the President several times, but was in no way an intimate friend or advisor.

Billy backed Kennedy's moves during the Cuban missile crisis of 1962, and made a public statement standing behind the referendum on Bible reading in the public schools.

Billy Graham took up arms against one of the pet programs of the New Frontier in 1963, at the Los Angeles Crusade, when he said: "The Peace Corps is almost completely materialistic in its aims. Without God at its center it cannot possibly accomplish all that we might hope for it."

R. Sargent Shriver, head of the Peace Corps, termed Billy's remarks "unfortunate." He pointed out that the Peace Corps had been endorsed by the Southern Baptist Convention, Billy's own denomination.

After Kennedy's assassination, Billy Graham was invited by Attorney General Robert F. Kennedy to sit in a special section at St. Matthew's Cathedral reserved for personal friends of the late President.

During Lyndon Johnson's Presidency Billy Graham visited the White House many times. They had known each other since the 1950s, and now became better friends than ever. The two had much in common—not only were they both Southerners, but President Johnson was a great-grandson of the evangelist Baines, who led General Sam Houston, the Texas hero, to Christ.

His friendship with the Democratic President brought him a great deal of critical mail from people who did not like Johnson's politics. Billy held a press conference in which he said that his association with the President did not imply politics. He said he tried to be friendly with people in both political parties. He mentioned his friendship with Vice-President Nixon.

By the middle of 1965 Billy Graham was being called "Chaplain of the White House" by facetious newspaper pundits. Billy was amused by the tag. He responded with a statement of admiration for the President, who, he said, in "many ways carries the heaviest load of any man since Lincoln."

He went on to say, "I think we need unity and should pray for the President that God will help him. I have a sense he is depending on God and looking for his guidance in many directions.

"No man can imagine the loneliness in which the President must make his decision," he concluded.

President Johnson and Lady Bird were the first White House residents ever to attend a Billy Graham Crusade when, in November that year, they went to hear him preach at the Astrodome in Houston.

Marianne Means, a columnist for a Washington newspaper, wrote about the relationship between the two men:

"It is understandable that they should get along well. For there is a great deal of preacher in Lyndon Johnson and a great deal of the politician in Billy Graham. Each, in his way, is a dedicated but utterly realistic man. They are both products of the Southern Bible Belt; they share a fervent homespun eloquence which has enabled them to stir the emotions of other men and rise to the peak of their professions."

In Johnson's last weekend at the White House, Billy Graham joined the President there, and he was chosen to offer the major prayer at Nixon's inauguration.

During the 1968 campaign he played a quite different role from that of the 1960 election. Just after Nixon was nominated, Billy Graham met with Nixon and key leaders in the party to discuss the Vice-Presidential nomination.

When Nixon asked Billy whom he suggested, he told him he would pick Senator Mark Hatfield, to "give balance to your ticket. First of all he's a great Christian leader. He's almost a clergyman. He's been an educator and has taken a more liberal stance on most issues than you, and I think the ticket needs that kind of a balance."

Nixon, of course, chose Spiro Agnew. On August 18, 1968, Billy announced that he would remain neutral in the campaign and stay out of politics.

In the letter he sent from BGEA headquarters, he further stated, "Naturally my convictions and sympathies are strong this year and it will be difficult to keep quiet when I feel so deeply! However, I am praying that the man of God's choice will be elected."

In September Billy and Nixon appeared together when the candidate attended the Pittsburgh Crusade. The Nixons were introduced by the evangelist, who praised Nixon for his "generosity, tremendous constraint of temper, and his integrity in totaling his golf score."

At the end of the service Nixon told the press, "This was one of the most moving religious experiences of my life." In order to make the whole thing seem neutral, Billy Graham read a wire from Hubert Humphrey in which the Democratic candidate expressed deep admiration for Graham's work and congratulated the evangelist on the Pittsburgh Crusade's "great success."

Friendship aside, Nixon was the kind of candidate that Billy genuinely thought was needed at this particular juncture in American life, according to Streiker and Strober in *Religion and the New Majority*.

*Time* magazine analyzed the two men:

> Like Nixon, Graham considers that the Supreme Court has "gone too far in favoring criminals." He supports Black Power, but only if it means "a feeling of self respect," not violence or civil disobedience. He believes that the demonstrators at the Democratic Convention in Chicago were "wonderful kids, idealists—but manipulated by a small, well-organized hard core that wanted a confrontation." The Chicago police over-reacted but "I don't know how some of the policemen restrained themselves that long."

Immediately after the election, Billy Graham was selected by the President-elect to handle the inauguration-day prayer.

In the six-hundred-word prayer, Billy gave thanks that "in Thy sovereignty Thou has permitted Richard Nixon to lead us at this momentous hour of history." He described how the "materialistic and permissive" winds that had been sown had brought "us a whirlwind of crime, division and rebellion."

After the prayer, Billy Graham was called the *"de facto* Presidential chaplain."

*Life* magazine editorialized: "The White House atmosphere will be in part one of deliberate reflection. But the omnipresence of evangelist Billy Graham means that the idealism which will emerge is bound to have the urgency and the overtones of evangelism."

Reinhold Niebuhr attacked the "Nixon-Graham doctrine" which suggested that a spiritual solution had to be found for the problems of America.

He chastised the evangelist for his undue confidence in conversion, pointing out that in Neibuhr's opinion it obscured "the dual individual and social character of human selves and the individual and social character of their virtues and vices."

When Nixon instituted religious services at the White

House, Billy was the first speaker. In all, he presided over three White House services during Nixon's Presidency. His last was the December 1973 meeting at the height of the Watergate controversy, just before the President's resignation.

Prior to that, in 1970, Nixon had twice apparently used his friendship with Billy Graham to bolster his own image.

The first time was in May, when Nixon flew to Knoxville to share the stage with Billy at a religious service on the University of Tennessee campus. Nixon praised the evangelist: "All men share respect for the message he brings because what he will say to you is what America and the world needs to hear."

Nixon's appearance was coupled with that of Republican senatorial candidate William E. Brock III, campaigning against Senator Albert Gore, who was not there, although he represented Tennessee in the Senate.

The service was interrupted by a loud antiwar demonstration aimed at the President's Vietnam policy. However, Billy Graham remained purposeful and deliberate in his integration stance. As the hundreds came forward to receive Christ, he challenged them "to return to the office, shop or school and love the person of another race."

Nixon's second opportunity came at the appearance of Billy Graham at the Honor America Day observance on the Fourth of July. Hobart Lewis, president of *Reader's Digest,* and Billy Graham had conceived the program in an attempt to try to drum up confidence in "the institutions of America" by bringing all people together for their country. Lewis and the evangelist brought in Bob Hope to help initiate the program.

The celebration was an attempt to bring together pro- and antiwar forces for the good of America. The antiwar forces wouldn't join in. Nevertheless, in front of the Lincoln Memorial on July 4, Billy pleaded with Americans to avoid the cries of extremists and stop the polarization "before it is too late."

After enumerating the positive reasons for America's

greatness and pointing out its current negative aspects, he said:

"Let's dedicate ourselves to a renewal of faith in God, equality, justice and peace for all. Let's dedicate ourselves to building rather than burning. I am asking all Americans today, especially our young people, to pursue this vision under God, to work for freedom and peace, to labor relentlessly, to love passionately, to serve selflessly, to pray earnestly and to die nobly if need be. I say to you today: Pursue the vision, reach toward the goal, fulfill the dream, and as you move to do it, never give in! Never give in!"

According to Streiker and Strober, "Graham was suggesting a way out of the wilderness, a path not like the straight and narrow where Southern strategy and Northeastern radicalism could prosper, but the broad path which could lead in 1972 to political success if those who have ears to hear would pause to listen."

The convulsions of Watergate soon occupied the minds of everyone in the administration and in America itself. The Vietnam War was phased out, but the polarization continued. Now a split between the government officials and the people themselves became evident.

In a public statement in 1974, Billy Graham clarified his feelings about Watergate and the President's actions.

"I can make no excuse for Watergate," he said. "The actual break-in was a criminal act, and some of the things that surround Watergate were not only unethical but criminal. I condemn it and I deplore it. It has hurt America."

When asked why he did not censure the President personally for his actions, he said: "A pastor tries to encourage and help a man in trouble, and to lead him out of it."

President Nixon's enemies accused the President of "using" Billy Graham's friendship in order to give him respectability.

"In 1960," Billy stated, "Nixon told me not to endorse him. 'Billy, your ministry is more important than my election to the Presidency.'"

The real problem, Billy said, was the absence in America of an absolute standard of right and wrong. The absence of that standard contributed to wrongdoing in office, such as the criminal acts related to the Watergate break-in.

"We've been told by popular theologians for some years that morals are determined by the situation, and now we are reaping the bitter fruits of that teaching," Billy Graham said.

"Some of the men involved in Watergate practiced that kind of ethics. If God is, then what God says must be absolute—man must have moral boundaries. He cannot devise his own morals to fit his own situation.

"The Bible tells us that with what judgment we judge we shall be judged. So we must avoid hypocritical and self-righteous glee at the evil that has been done.

"The Bible also teaches us, 'Lie not one to another.' There is no blinking the fact that Watergate has become a symbol of political corruption and evil. But let us hope that by God's grace we may turn the corner.

"Let's hope we realize that there is one crisis more urgent than the energy crisis and that this is the crisis in integrity and in Christian love and in forgiveness."

# CHAPTER NINETEEN

# Civil Rights

By the early 1960s Billy Graham had added Howard Jones of Cleveland to integrate his team. Later, he brought in Ralph Bell, a graduate of Taylor University.

"We've held integrated crusades in every Southern state except Georgia, Alabama, and Mississippi," Billy stated in a *Reader's Digest* article, "and have not had a single incident."

He went on to decry segregation within the American church:

"How does one explain why, of all of America's great institutions, the Christian Church is still the most segregated? It has become a byword that 'the most segregated hour of the week is still eleven o'clock Sunday morning.' This is true of churches in the North as well as in the South."

In the 1960s, civil rights developed into a full-fledged movement, with sit-ins and demonstrations being reported by the national press and being supported by some moderates as well as liberals.

On May 17, 1961, Freedom Riders were attacked in Anniston and Montgomery, Alabama, with violence inflicting injuries on the participants.

Billy Graham urged that the culprits be prosecuted to the full extent of the law. "I think it is deplorable when certain people in any society have been treated as second-class citizens," he said on May 18.

He also spoke out in Little Rock and New Orleans, when the situation was particularly tense. After a racist's bomb had blown up a school in Clinton, Tennessee, he made another strong statement to the press. And he spoke out in Birmingham, Alabama, in direct defiance of threatening letters and telephone calls.

In 1963, after the murders in Selma and Montgomery, Alabama, Billy took his most determined stand. At the time he was ill in a hospital in Honolulu.

A protest march had been organized by Dr. Martin Luther King, Jr., to point up the fact that blacks in Selma made up half the population but had only one percent of the vote.

Major John McCloud of the Alabama State Police ordered the marchers to go back to their church. They simply stood there in silence, without offering any resistance.

The state troopers, in concert with a posse of citizens from Selma and a number of sheriff's deputies, rushed the group, beating them with clubs and tossing tear gas into their ranks.

The protesters were effectively dispersed.

That was not the end of the trouble. With violence simmering always just below the surface, both blacks and whites walked on eggs, eyeing each other for several days.

Then, two nights later, the Reverend James Reeb and two other ministers were attacked in front of the Silver Moon Café by whites. They were beaten up in a most deliberate and determined fashion. Reeb died of his wounds.

Billy Graham, recuperating in his hospital bed in Honolulu, had been following the sequence of events by way of radio news flashes. He telephoned his Atlanta headquarters and gave orders to two of his close associates to get over to Selma and other Alabama cities to organize meetings.

Dr. Walter Herbert Smythe and Stanley Monneyham did as instructed, putting together groups of church-going people to try to cool down the tense situation.

Ten days after Reeb died, a civil rights march from Selma to Montgomery was instituted by Dr. King. The march was fraught with danger, and was watched carefully by Ku Kluxers and other militant racists in Alabama.

King took with him a blind man, a nun, a cripple, and a score or more of ministers of the Gospel. There were also groups of civil rights workers marching with King's nucleus.

They reached Montgomery on March 25. The town had been alerted to trouble by the Justice Department in Washington under Robert F. Kennedy and by other citizens concerned with the safety of the marchers.

The Montgomery police were not adequately reinforced to handle trouble. And trouble came. A group of Ku Klux Klan members, running with other white right-wingers, attacked the marchers in the middle of the town.

Mrs. Viola Liuzzo, a civil rights worker, was murdered in the ensuing pitched battle. Scores of others were injured.

Billy announced that he was moving his Crusade team into Alabama.

Although it takes about eight to twenty months to organize a Crusade, the Graham team was able to get the Alabama Crusade mounted within five weeks after the death of Mrs. Liuzzo.

On Saturday, May 1, Billy spoke in Dothan, Alabama, where his brother-in-law was pastor of the Presbyterian church.

While there, he announced a ten-day Crusade in Montgomery starting in June. During his sermon he denounced racial discrimination as a product of man's sinfulness. He pointed out that he had refused to speak before segregated groups during that time.

Liberals among the civil rights advocates were quoted as "skeptical" about Billy's type of preaching. They preferred picket lines to words.

"I think my ministry is a little bit different from marching," Billy told the press. "I believe the church must cleanse itself before attacking secular ills."

In an aside to the media, Billy discussed the need for racial understanding. However, he informed them that he would continue in the pulpit to offer his people the message of the Gospel on race.

"I believe that under the shadows of the cross of Christ is the true place of true brotherhood," he said. He would, he promised, continue not to harangue, but bring the word of the Bible to his supporters.

He was quoted as saying that a true conversion to Christ inevitably affects man's racial attitude. *Time* magazine commented:

"His kind of preaching may have special value in the South, where both white and Negro share a common tradition of reverence for gospel-centered Christianity."

Billy himself told the *Time* man that despite "huge psychological barriers," he believed that the South might overcome its difficulties before the North did.

"We're building for future generations," he said. "Younger people look at things differently now."

He was given a great press by the newspapers and wire services, and by the news magazines. On the following Monday, he preached at the University of Alabama, where, some time earlier, Governor George Wallace had stood with his back to the door to keep two black students from enrolling. Wallace's defiance was, of course, a symbolic gesture and nothing more; the University of Alabama had been integrated within hours with the help of the federal government.

Next morning Billy held a rally at Auburn University, and that night he spoke at Tuskegee Institute. In June he returned to Alabama after a commitment in Denmark, and opened a Montgomery Crusade. He spoke there for several days, and in some cases several times during each day.

"At any one of those meetings he could have been murdered," wrote Alan Bestic, "for any Southerner who preached integration is a quisling in the eyes of white supremists."

Bestic continued, "There at any rate was a splendid, blood-and-guts Graham." And finally, "His voice is powerful, though here I am not referring to its decibel content."

In September Billy said that if clergymen of both races would invite him to, he would hold an integrated crusade in Birmingham. The invitation was not forthcoming.

In the same month, the Sixteenth Street Baptist Church in Birmingham was bombed by racists. Four Negro girls were killed. A biracial committee of Protestant, Roman Catholic, and Jewish laymen invited Billy Graham to preach to an audience in Birmingham.

On Easter Sunday, 1964, Billy Graham made history by preaching to an integrated audience of fifty thousand blacks and whites in Birmingham's Legion Field.

He called for a new effort by all men to end prejudice in America. His message accentuated national issues, but it was obvious that he was speaking to the citizens of Birmingham about Birmingham's problems.

Standing on the platform just below the Negro section of the city called "Dynamite Hill" by its inhabitants, he said:

"What a moment and what an hour for Birmingham. It is good to stand together for Christ."

The Reverend J. L. Ware, a Negro clergyman, said at the end of the service that the session may have opened up the beginning of a new period of racial peace in the Alabama city.

Billy's view of the racial crisis was analyzed through the context of human values.

"We are now beginning to realize that something is desperately wrong with human nature. The most burning question of our times is the problem of man. What causes the hate, prejudice, lust, immorality, greed, deceit, fraud, and war that we read and hear about each day?"

He said, "We must preach the Gospel of Christ, not race; such efforts can be of immense help in this racial misunderstanding."

It was obvious that Billy understood completely the implications of the fact that he had been invited to Birmingham not by churchmen but by laymen.

Next day, speaking to a meeting of the National

Association of Evangelicals, he pleaded with evangelical leaders to assume greater responsibility for solving the racial crisis.

"We should have been leading the way to racial justice, but we failed; let's confess it, let's admit it, and let's do something about it."

Next month, in May 1964, speaking at the University of North Carolina, he made what most believed to be his strongest statement on race:

"Those people who say they can prove segregation from the Bible don't know their Bible." He explained that the real message of the Bible was to "love thy neighbor as thyself."

The crisis of a long, hot, bloody summer could be resolved only "when the hearts of men and women have been transformed and made to love instead of hate."

His basic theme was:

"America has to get back to God in the next five or six years or we will face troubles and bloodshed such as you cannot dream about in your suburban homes."

In the fall of 1964 he became convinced that the South was probably nearer to solving its race problems than the North:

"The South has few ghettoes and is making rapid progress toward integration."

In Boston he said, "In the South there is real friendship upon which to build a solution to the problem. In the North you have *de facto* segregation and this is much harder to overcome."

In March 1965 he urged President Johnson to meet with leaders on both sides of the rapidly escalating Alabama civil rights crisis. In April he canceled several engagements in Great Britain in order to hold meetings in Alabama, to which he had been invited by white and black clergymen.

At one of the meetings a Baptist layman admitted that he had been prejudiced against blacks all his life, but he was now convinced that "if we are to win the world for Christ, we're going to have to be color blind."

The series of meetings got Billy national headlines, with the *New York Times* carrying a long article: "Billy Graham Is Focusing on Rights."

In the article, the reporter quoted Billy in a restatement of his belief that the Bible did not support segregation or bar intermarriage. And he was quoted as being in favor of the Civil Rights Act of 1964 and rights legislation then in the works in Washington.

As for the demonstrators, "I never felt that we should attain our rights by illegal means, yet I must confess that the demonstrations have served to arouse the conscience of the world."

Later in the year, at a Crusade in Montgomery, the evangelist spoke to a hundred thousand residents in the first biracial event in the capital's history. "Night after night," he said, "I watched hundreds of people of both races march not with hatred but in unity and a spirit of love as Christ drew them together."

He concluded, "If the Ku Klux Klan will give Alabama time to digest the new civil rights laws, and if the politicians will not try to exploit the situation, progress will continue."

Two months later Watts, the black section in south central Los Angeles, blew up. When the riots broke out, Billy flew to Los Angeles.

In L.A. he got "first-class, red-carpet briefing" from state, city and National Guard officials, led by Governor Edmund Brown.

Donning a bulletproof vest, Billy viewed the riot area from the protected seat of a police helicopter. He concluded that extremists had played a major role in leading the disturbance.

"I believe the riots have hurt the civil rights cause. People across the nation are afraid, baffled, and bewildered by what happened in Los Angeles."

Through the rest of 1965, he stressed that theme. He continued on into the following year, pointing out: "The majority of the American people want law, order, and security in our society. There is no doubt that the rioting, looting, and crime in America this summer has reached the point of anarchy."

With the last of the 1960s, the riots ended and the Black Power movement faded out. But the problem of civil rights was not yet solved. And Billy Graham's attitude is that there is really only one way to solve it. As he wrote in *The Presbyterian Journal:*

"The only way to change men is to get them converted to Jesus Christ. Then they will have the capacity to live up to the Christian command: 'love thy neighbor.' "

# CHAPTER TWENTY

# The Sermon

Even from the first days in Tampa when he preached on a cypress stump to frogs and alligators, Billy Graham has always concentrated a great deal on the subject matter of the sermon he preaches and the manner in which he presents it.

A sermon may start out like this:

"We are here tonight by divine appointment. We are here to meet God and His Son, Jesus Christ. Let us open our hearts to receive Him."

Billy has always believed in speaking in short sentences and clear phrases. He has never believed in obfuscation and confusion. Because he believes in God and in Jesus Christ and in the words of the Bible, he wants to communicate his belief directly to his audience.

He may go on:

"God has a plan for your life. It was set up before you were born. The blueprints are in heaven and are gone over carefully. You can ignore the plan and go to hell. Or you can put yourself in God's hand so that you can follow the life that has been planned for you. The choice is yours."

Again, he believes in using familiar everyday concepts—the blueprint—to show what he wants to show. Nor is he afraid of superlatives: heaven, hell. His words are direct and challenging.

And he may continue:

"Are you getting what you want out of life? Christ died to atone for your sins. If you are willing to be

183

reborn as a child, Christ will carry your burdens. He loves you. He wants you to shift your burdens to His shoulders. You will never have to suffer another defeat. You can go from victory to victory to victory!"

The message is clear. There is no backing and filling, no doubting and fearing. The choice is clear. The message: Make your choice and take it.

Once the sermon is under way, Billy then takes some Biblical story—the Flood, the Prodigal Son, Daniel in the Lions' Den—and relates modern life to the Biblical story.

For example:

> So this giant Goliath was out challenging all the armies of Israel, and everybody was afraid. David was watching the sheep. He wasn't even old enough to go to war. His brothers had gone to fight. They weren't doing much fighting. They were just sitting around listening to a big giant brag, and they were all scared to death.
>
> So David's father came to him and said, "Son, I want you to go out to the armies and take some grain and some bread out there and give it to your brothers. They are probably hungry." So David went out with the bread and the grain and when he arrived there with these provisions, he heard this big giant. The ground almost shook at the power of his voice.
>
> He said, "I defy the armies of Israel. Send a man out here to fight me."
>
> And David said, "Who in the world is that fellow defying the armies of the Lord God? Who is that guy?"
>
> They said, "He's Goliath." They said, "He's the biggest man in the world; the most powerful man in the world."
>
> David said, "Why doesn't someone go fight him?"
>
> They said, "We're all scared. We'd never win. He'd kill us all."
>
> David looked at him and said, "I'll fight him."

And his brothers laughed at him and sneered and mocked, and the whole group of soldiers laughed.

"Huh, a boy like you going out to fight a giant like that? Are you crazy? Don't make a fool of yourself trying to show off."

He said, "Take me to King Saul. I volunteer to fight the giant."

So they took him to King Saul, and King Saul said, "Well, you're just a boy. I can't send you out there to fight Goliath. Why, the greatest warriors we've got are afraid of him. He'll cut your head off with that giant sword of his."

David said, "Sir, Your Majesty, out yonder while I was watching my sheep a bear came out. It killed the sheep. With my bare hands God helped me to kill the bear. A lion came out to grab one of our sheep one day, and God helped me to vanquish the lion with my bare hands. And the same God that helped me in the fight with the bear and helped me in the fight with the lion is going to help me with the fight with Goliath, because Goliath should not be allowed to defy the armies of the Lord God."

Saul said, "All right, if you are determined to go, go ahead. But you don't have any army, you don't have a sword, you don't have any weapons . . ."

Now David had a strong faith. It must have taken a lot of faith out there with that bear. We've got bears down where I live, and I wouldn't want to go out and face one of them. So it must have taken a lot of faith. Tarzan had a knife, but David didn't even have a knife when he faced that lion, but he whipped the lion. Now, have you ever tried to beard a lion and wrestle with him? Well, that's what David did.

You see, his spiritual strength had been developed in secret and nourished in solitude. He had made his decision to life for God out under the stars and out on the desert, and he determined that he was going to serve God at an early age.

So David went out, and he did an interesting thing.

He had a slingshot and he stopped at a brook and picked up five stones. Somebody asked why he had five stones; he only needed one. Someone has pointed out that Goliath had four relatives, and David had a stone for every one of them.

Now, David was without experience. Goliath had more experience than he did. David was outnumbered, because Goliath had his armor bearer. He was outarmed, he was outweighed, but David said, "You come to me with a sword. You come to me with a shield and a spear, but I come to you in the name of the Lord of Hosts. I come to you in God's name."

And the Bible says that he took that slingshot, he put a stone in it, and flung the stone at Goliath. The great giant had a look of surprise on his face; a thought entered his mind that had never been there before. That stone went right into his brain, and he crumpled and fell—dead. God had delivered the giant by the little David with a slingshot.

Now that story applies to you spiritually. There are many giants in your life. You've got some big giants, hangups. I want to tell you that with faith in Christ, with Christ in your heart, you can go out and you can defeat the biggest giant in the world.

Although the story is a modernized version of the Biblical story, it is simply embellished to bring out the dramatic moments of the original narrative. And the point is underlined time and again, showing that faith can help the small man conquer big problems.

This type of sermon is quite different from the earlier sermons Billy used to deliver. And his style of preaching has changed, too.

Stanley High wrote that he once played a recording from Billy Graham's early days as a preacher. What was preached was almost lost in the way it was preached:

"His voice was strident. He was inclined to rant. The

same sound effects in politics would, in most places, be called demagoguery."

High was reminded of Billy Sunday: coat off, tie off, face dripping sweat, down on all fours, peering over the edge of the platform as into a fiery pit, shouting, in raw and rasping voice, his defiance of the hosts of hell.

Billy's sermons now are smooth and slow, and his gestures, which used to be sharp and theatrical, are quite subdued.

As for subject matter, take, for example, an early version of Daniel in the Lions' Den and compare it to the preceding story of David and Goliath.

Daniel was the prime minister of one of the powerful countries in the world and a pal of the boss—the King of the Medes and Persians. Some jealous guys were out to get him, so they trained their spyglass on him one morning when he was praying and had his venetian blinds up. They tattled to the King. The King was on the spot, so he said to his lawyers: "Find me a couple of loopholes so I can spring my pal, Dan." They just couldn't find a loophole, and the King just had to send Dan to the lions.

So, what happens? Old Daniel walks in. He's not afraid. He looks the first big cat in the eye and kicks him and says, "Move over there, Leo. I want a nice fat lion with a soft belly for a pillow, so I can get a good night's rest . . ."

And so on.

Billy used to speak on the radio like Walter Winchell, whom he deliberately emulated. But lately he has slowed down some.

His gestures have toned down, but not that much. During his usual sermon, he moves from one gesture to another without pause. In a familiar series of moves, he lifts up the open Bible, first in one hand and then in the other, sometimes with both, holding it aloft, as someone has said, "like a pizza from a hot oven."

A writer once clocked twenty-one gestures in the space of little more than a minute; as Stanley High quoted them: "arms flailing, arms folded, arms akimbo, fists clenched, palms opened, slapping the Bible, the pulpit, the platform railing, finger pointing to Heaven, to Hell, at you."

With the coming of television, Billy's gestures have been trimmed almost to nothing. High was writing about Billy in the 1950s. When Billy speaks to foreign audiences, he stands beside a translator and simply delivers his sentences first, without excessive gestures, and the translator repeats them.

His style of writing has changed, too. Edward B. Fiske, formerly religion editor of the *New York Times*, discussed Billy's preaching in 1970:

"He no longer draws vivid verbal pictures of the fires of hell, nor does he still assert that heaven is sixteen hundred miles in each direction." However, Fiske adds, "He is still willing to describe in detail the way in which Christ will return to earth and rule for a thousand years."

What exactly does Billy Graham believe? He believes that the Bible is God's word. He believes that every truth can be found in its writings.

"I do believe this," he said. "I believe the Bible is God's holy and inspired word. I accept the Apostles' Creed one hundred percent. Many liberals don't. They do not believe that Jesus was born of a virgin. I do. They do not believe that Christ was raised bodily from the dead. I do. They do not believe He will come again, in glory, to judge the world. I do. But I don't try to predict the day and hour of His coming, as some preachers have done to their sorrow, for I don't know the day and hour. Nobody does."

In a speech to the Harvard Divinity School in February 1964, Billy Graham said:

"I used to think that in evangelism I had to do it all, but now I approach evangelism with a totally different attitude. I approach it with complete relaxation. First of all, I don't believe any man can come to Christ unless the Holy Spirit has prepared his heart. Secondly, I don't believe any man can come to Christ unless God draws him. My job is to proclaim the message. It's the Holy Spirit's job to do the work. And so I approach it with a great deal of relaxation now.

"When I see 100 or 500 people, or whatever number it may be, respond to an appeal to receive Christ, I know that in that group are certain people whose lives will be irrevocably changed from that moment on. And I have that confidence every time I preach.

"I believe, with all my heart as I look back on my life, that I was chosen to do this particular work as a man might have been chosen to go into East Harlem and work there, or to the slums of London like General Booth. I believe that God in His sovereignty—I have no other answer for this—sheer sovereignty, chose me to do this work and prepared me in His own way."

The gist of the message Billy Graham preaches is this: "Man rebelled against God, and so he was separated from God by sin. Christ died, was buried, and He rose again, and men need to repent of their sins and receive Him as their Savior."

# CHAPTER TWENTY-ONE

# The Wisdom of Billy Graham

The Bible says God Almighty created the human race for a special purpose. God is love. He wanted some other creature in the universe like Himself, made in His image, little gods who had a will of their own who could return love to Him.

God was lonely; God craved and wanted fellowship. Incredible as that sounds, God wanted fellowship.

He wanted somebody to love Him and He created the human race and put them on this planet. He said if you will obey the moral laws of the universe, we will walk together and build a wonderful and beautiful world together. But if you rebel against this, if you break the moral laws, you will suffer and die and be judged.

In every phase of life we face this recurring question: "What think ye of Christ?" In youth, too happy to think—I've plenty of time. In manhood, too busy to think—I must make a living. In maturity, too anxious to think—I've more urgent problems. Declining years, too old to think—my pattern of life is set. As death approaches, too ill to think—my sensibilities are dulled and my mind weary. Death, too late to think—the spirit is flown, the day of opportunity is past, the harvest is gone, and now God's Judgment Day.

There are three little men that live down inside of every one of us. One is intellect, another is emotion and the third is will. Intellectually, you may accept Christ. Emotionally, you may feel that you can love

Him. However, until you have surrendered to Christ by a definite act of your will, you are not a Christian.

The Gulf Stream is the ocean, and yet it is not a part of it. Believers are in the world, and yet they must not be absorbed by it. The Gulf Stream maintains its warm temperatures even in the icy water of the North Atlantic. If Christians are to fulfill their purposes in the world they must not be chilled by the indifferent, godless society in which they live.

Newton had his dynamics of matter and motion. Einstein had his dynamics of relativity. But Jesus Christ has His dynamics of the Spirit. In chemistry, under given conditions, hydrogen and oxygen combine to form water. So repentance and faith in Christ produce a new life.

You may be able to pronounce all the shibboleths. You may be able to pronounce all the clichés. You may be able to split all the theological hairs. You may be a theological bloodhound, but I tell you tonight, unless we are separated from the temper and lusts and evils of the world, we cannot call ourselves God's children.

The Bible is the constitution of Christianity. Just as the United States Constitution is not of any private interpretation, neither is the Bible of any private interpretation. Just as the Constitution includes all who live under its stated domain, without exception, so the Bible includes all who live under its stated domain, without exception. As the Constitution is absolute, so the Bible is absolute. As the Constitution is the highest law of man, so the Bible is the highest law of God. God's laws for the spiritual world are found in the Bible. Whatever else there may be that tells us of God, it is more clearly told in the Bible.

A man who is unfaithful to his wife in thought, word or deed has committed one of the greatest crimes known to God and man. It is one of the few sins for which God demanded the death penalty in the Old Testament. God says that no adulterer will be found in the Kingdom of Heaven. The wrath of God is waiting at the Judgment Day for any man who is unfaithful to his wife and guilty of this terrible sin. If you have committed this sin, renounce it, and then confess it to God; the Bible says, "If we confess our sins, He is faithful and just to forgive us our sins" (1 John 1:9). Yes, it is possible for you to be forgiven and cleansed at this moment.

Take time to spend with your children. Give them ideals, morals and spiritual values; set a good example; plan family activities as a unit; discipline yourselves and your children. But most of all, teach them to know God through regular family prayer; Bible reading and church attendance also help.

I heard about a father who gave his boy an unusual Christmas present. He wrapped a note in a package; the note read: "Son, during the next year I am going to give you one hour every day and two hours on Sunday." The little boy ran and put his arm around his dad and said, "Oh, Dad, that's the best Christmas present I've ever had."

Your children not only require a great deal of your time, they long and hunger for it. Perhaps they do not express it, but the hunger and longing are there just the same. Be a pal to your children, love them, spend hours with them. Cut out some of your so-called important social engagements and make your home the center of your social life. God will honor you and your children will grow up to call you "blessed."

It is not so much a problem of what is right and what is wrong as of who decides what is right and what is wrong. No longer does the teen-ager know who his master is. Everywhere I travel I find that young people want to know: "Is there a final authority?" "Is there any objective source for authority?" When young people are left to themselves to make their own moral choices, they flounder. They are not ready for the big decisions of life. They need authority. They are insecure without it. Something inside the young person cries out in longing for someone to tell him with authority that this is right and that is wrong.

Although many do not realize it, youth demands authority. Many parents and teachers fail to realize that youth responds to rules, regulations and discipline. Without this, they are confused and bewildered.

. . . Today's parents have helped to create the background for their children's rebellion. Many parents imply that being popular is more important than being honest, that being busy is more important than being together, that owning a car is more important than respecting another's property. Some parents stay so busy with activities outside the home that their children are forced to get just as busy themselves or be alone. Other parents are in a constant frenzy, organizing activities for their children so that they don't have a free moment. As a result, young people have no time to get acquainted with their parents—or with themselves.

Too much emphasis is exerted both at home and at school in trying to make adults out of sub-teen-agers and small children. We are told that these subteens should be prepared for adjustments to adult life. But studies indicate that they are being robbed of their childhood. From both their teachers and their parents these young people are being given a false sense of values, with the result that they become psychologically and emotionally unstable.

Throughout the behavior of parents, teachers and teen-agers alike there seems to run the theme of freedom from responsibility, which leads directly to rebellion.

Young people are rebelling, but they are tragically without a cause. They are searching for a creed to believe, a song to sing, a flag to follow and a slogan to shout. If our youth could know the security, the joy and the challenge of commitment to Christ, the nation and the world could be changed.

Do you know what nearly all the sociologists say today in their study of young people? The greatest problem facing young people today is not sex, it is boredom, boredom. Did you know that when they had the riot at Hampton Beach in New Hampshire they asked the young people what was wrong, why did they do it? "Just for the hell of it." Bored—life has no purpose, life has no meaning. Give your life to Christ and you will never spend another bored minute.

Separation of Church and state was never meant to separate schoolchildren from God! This trend to extricate God and moral teachings from the school is a diabolical scheme, and is bearing its fruit in the deluge of juvenile delinquency that is overwhelming our nation!

We are rich in the things that perish, but poor in the things of the spirit. We are rich in gadgets, but poor in faith. We are rich in goods, but poor in grace. We are rich in know-how, but poor in character. We are rich in words, but poor in deeds. We say we are rich, but in God's estimate we are wretched, miserable, poor, blind and naked.

We must face it. We've lost God. We've lost our contact with the Almighty. We've lost our anchorage; we've lost our moorings; we've lost our contact with the supernatural, with the harmonizer and coordinator of the universe. There is a lack of sense of life in America today.

In a decadent society the will to believe, to resist, to contend, to fight, to struggle, is gone. In place of this will to resist there is the desire to conform, to drift, to follow, to yield and to give up. This is what happened to Rome, but it also applies to us. The same conditions that prevailed in Rome prevail in our society. Before Rome fell, her standards were abandoned, the family disintegrated, divorce prevailed, immorality was rampant and faith was at a low ebb. As Gibbon said, "There was much talk of religion, but few practiced it." Today our churches are filled, but how many are actually practicing Christianity in daily life?

The Athenians were proud. They thought no one was superior to them, and we have today our social snobbery, our intellectual pride and our racial superiority.

But God says we come from the same blood. We had the same first parents. Whether your skin is dark or light, no matter what shape and size you may be, we are all the same in God's sight. We come from the same blood.

Racial tension today is increasing in the world. In some areas it is already flaming into underground warfare. Being born black in some parts of the world, Jewish in other parts, or Oriental in others, or white in some places, imposes burdens while those who are accidentally born in the ruling majority enjoy advantages they have not always earned, and for which they have little appreciation.

To hate, to discriminate against those who look different, who talk different, who have different national backgrounds or who act differently from the dominant group is a universal trait of human nature. Racial prejudice is not limited to the southern part of the United States or South Africa. I have observed it all over the world. Where two races live side by side, there exists prejudice.

. . . I say today there is only one possible solution and that is a vital experience with Christ on the part of both races. In Christ the middle wall of partition is broken down, the Bible says. There is no Jew or Gentile or black or white or yellow or red. We could be one great brotherhood in Christ.

However, until we come to recognize Him as the

Prince of Peace and receive His love in our hearts, the racial tensions will increase.

This wave of bombing which is taking place in schools and synagogues and churches is symptomatic of the very things that brought Hitler to power in Germany a few years ago.

I think that every Christian should deplore it, whatever we think about the race problem. All of us are opposed to sticks of dynamite being thrown at churches and synagogues and schools, endangering lives. I am sure we are all opposed to violence; and I think that you would join me in saying tonight that we ought to pray that this spirit of restlessness and hatred and bitterness will somehow be brought to an end, because this could become very serious.

This could eventually lead to the forces of crime and the hate groups in this country taking advantage of a crisis, which could lead to anarchy and Communism.

The crack in the moral dam is widening, but [as with] the people of Noah's day before the Flood, life goes on as usual, with only a few concerned and only a minority alarmed. However, apathy will not deter catastrophe. The people of Noah's day were not expecting judgment, but it came. We have become soft and comfortable. Watching television, I notice that when any crisis arises on the screen, the actor usually says, "Give me a drink." When the headlines get black, the sale of alcohol and barbiturates rises in the country as millions try to escape from the grim realities of our dangers.

There is no doubt that evil in the world is becoming more intensified. Satan is accelerating his activities because he realizes that the time is short. The seeds of evil are propagated from parent to child, with each little one bringing into the world as his spiritual inheritance a propensity for evil which mingles with all his propensities for good. Each new life seems to bring a fresh contribution to the already abundant growth of evil. It is a mere germ at first, expressing itself in rebellion against the mother, the slapping at the father, the tendency toward lying and the rebellion against all authority on the part of young children.

If early in life the child does not have a personal encounter with the Lord Jesus Christ, then evil sinks its fangs deep into the bloodstream and injects its terrifying poison. This poison is active, subtle, swift and successful. Its results are catastrophic. It affects the mind, the conscience, and most of all, the will. The mind is blinded, the conscience is deadened and the will is paralyzed.

However, there is a wonderful cure for this disease. So you today with sin in your heart can be saved by the blood of Christ. Your sins can be washed away. You can have a new nature. You can have Christ actually living in your heart. And it is only as we individuals come to Jesus Christ that we can make an impact on our society and roll back the tide of evil that seeks to engulf us.

Immorality, which is the sin of perversion and unnaturalness, has a way of making those who harbor it unnaturally-appearing. The shifty eyes, the suggestive glance—these are marks of the impure. They are the outward signs of inward impurities. But the outward marks are slight compared to the blemishes which impurity etches upon the soul. Guilt complexes and bad conscience are fashioned in the fires of lustful passion. Out of unbalanced practices of impurity grow phobias which alarm even our most skilled psychiatrists.

When you come to know Christ, there dwells within you the Holy Spirit. Who gives you supernatural strength to overcome temptation and evil, so that when you face it, you don't face it alone. The Spirit of God gives you the power to say no.

All of us are tempted. If you have not been tempted you are the only one in the world. Even Christ was

tempted. But the Bible teaches that temptation is not a
sin. Many Christians become confused at this point.
They are tempted, they think the temptation is itself a
sin, and so they get discouraged and go ahead and sin.
But the sin comes only when we yield to the temptation.

Another sin of the tongue that is prevalent among
Christians is the sin of criticism—going around and
trying to take a speck out of our brother's eye when
we have a log in our own.

Sin pays—but it pays off in remorse, regret and
failure.

There are evidences of [a] lost sense of sin in thousands of facets of our modern life. It is evident in the
increase of profanity and obscenity. Our depraved
speech is a direct reflection of our depraved lives. Our
lost sense of sin is evidenced by our accent on pleasure.
The hue and cry of today is "Let us eat, drink and be
merry, for tomorrow we die." We are becoming a
nation of Playboys and are debasing the wisdom God
has given us upon the altars of appetite and desire. We
are becoming wise to do evil.

Our lost sense of sin is evidenced by our unnatural
emphasis upon sex. The sin of impurity does not appear ugly and venomous at first. It comes in the guise
of beauty, symmetry and desirability. There is nothing
repulsive about it. Satan clothes his goddess of lust as
an angel of love, and her appearance has deceived the
strongest of men. God hates this unnatural emphasis
on sex in America. It has caused nations to fall. It
has over and over ruined the sanctity of the home. It
has caused the spiritual downfall of thousands.

The sex revolution that has been taking place, especially in the United States during the last twenty-five
years, is changing the lives of men and women more
radically than any other revolution in history. The
revolution drastically affects the lives of millions, deeply

disturbs the community and decisively influences the future of society. Some of our professors of psychology and sociology are teaching that the sex drive is the vital mainstream of human behavior. In the name of science, its fuller satisfaction is urged as a necessary condition of man's health and happiness. Sex inhibitions are viewed as the main source of frustration, mental and physical illness. Sexual chastity is ridiculed as a prudish superstition and marriage loyalty is stigmatized as antiquated hypocrisy.

Immorality and impurity have penetrated almost every area of our American culture. In the realm of literature there is growing preoccupation with the "sub-social sewers." Filthy, pornographic and obscene books are now on the shelves of most drugstores and newsstands throughout America. Millions of old and young alike are feeding on them every week. The beautiful moral literature of fifty years ago has been displaced by various forms of abnormal, perverse, vulgar, exotic and even monstrous forms.

The impure influence is also felt in the realm of music. Music has become seductive, sensual and perverse in the bulk of nightclub, television and radio entertainment.

Many church leaders are becoming alarmed about the tendency toward sex, filth, dirt, profanity and even perversion now on the screen in some of the newer films. A recent study disclosed that fifty-five percent of the topics of modern movies were devoted to sex, and about thirty-five percent to crime. In fact, a few movies have become so frankly pornographic that they have provoked open protest from various organizations and communities.

Many church leaders now advocate a so-called new morality. What they propose is a standard based on love without law, in which the ultimate criterion for right and wrong is not the command of God, but the individual's subjective perception of what is good for himself and his neighbor in each given situation. In my opinion, this is not a new morality—this is the old morality.

Now, every young person in the audience tonight has that problem [sex] because God gave you the gift of sex. There's nothing wrong with it. It is given by God, and the Bible doesn't adopt a "hush-hush" attitude toward it. The Bible speaks plainly about it, and sex in its God-given place can be one of the greatest servants in the world, but it can be a terrible tyrant.

God says that the place for sex is within the marriage. Before marriage, take this gift, dedicate it to God, and it will become a dynamo in your life, that will take you to the top of anything.

Today a spell of doom and dismay has settled down upon the hearts of men. No matter where we travel the specter of hopelessness is found. We see it in bold type in the headlines of the papers. We see it in the deep lines that furrow troubled brows. We sense it in man's futile search for fulfillment. We see it in the purposelessness of living. The very atmosphere seems impregnated with a stifling hopelessness that has robbed millions of the zest for living.

Our world is very much like a man who has cancer. When cancer is brought under control in one spot, it often breaks out in another. The world specialists may employ all the diplomacy and skill at their command. They may, as the Bible says, "anoint themselves with the chief ointments," but at best they reach only symptoms, and the cleverest of this world's leaders have failed to diagnose the cause of the disease.

Nazism blossomed in Germany only after the church had failed to fill the vacuum following World War I. When the church failed to present and declare a dynamic living Christ, Germany was robbed of a Savior and gave birth to a dictator. When Christ is made to abdicate from His rightful place as Lord in any nation, tyranny takes over.

The leaders of the United Nations organization are blinded to the basic problem of the world. Thus they have no remedy. For centuries men have met, trying to solve the problems of the world in peace councils—the United Nations, the League of Nations and many other organizations. But they fail because they have never been able to accept the fact that man is basically a spiritual and moral failure. They never recognize the fact that we have sinned and rebelled against God and that our problem is not economic, but educational, not social, but spiritual and theological. Our problem is that we have a disease called sin.

And if every person in America would turn to Jesus Christ right now, our problem would be over tomorrow. Every national and international problem faced by man would be overcome tomorrow if we returned voluntarily to Jesus Christ, every one of them.

The church is on the tail end—to our shame!—of progress along racial lives in America today. The church should be leading instead of following.

I think that we in the church ought to lay down the guidelines for our leaders. Now, we have elected leaders to decide what to do about the political problems around the world. I don't think that I can sit in my home in North Carolina, without all the facts, and make statements about what we should do in these areas. I think we can preach the moral and spiritual guidelines that will help the President, the Secretary of State and some of these other people to decide, but these people have been elected, and they have the responsibility. And I am not sure that the church, as a church, ought to be specifying what to do about certain political situations in the world. I think that we can give general outlines, and moral guidance, but I don't think that we ought to specifically tell them. Now, for example, specifically, what to do about the problems in Asia.

The task as an evangelist is to plant the seed as a farmer would plant seed in the springtime. The farmer cannot make the seed grow, he cannot generate life—this can be done only by God. So when the seed is planted in the human heart, if other conditions are right, God will make the seed grow, causing that person to mature spiritually.

A hungry man is a dangerous man, and a man away from God can be plagued by phobias, fears and complexes. Why do people commit unthinkable crimes? Why do we have shocking episodes showing the bestiality of man? For the simple reason that men who have not had their basic needs met—the need of being reconciled to God—are unpredictable, untrustworthy, worried, anxious creatures. Of course, most people by sheer willpower are able to restrain themselves from gross crimes, but underneath the cloak of respectability seethes and surges a sinful nature that is capable of the worst evil imaginable. The very restraint exercised by modern man is one of the causes of tension and anxieties.

We live like a little ant on this little speck of dust out in space. We get a Ph.D. degree and we strut across the stage and say, "Well, I don't know whether there is a God or not." And we can't control ourselves.

We can't even keep from blowing ourselves apart. We can't even keep from manufacturing nuclear weapons that could destroy the world. We can't even keep from hating each other and fighting each other and killing each other.

We can't even keep from stealing from each other.

We can't even keep from dying, because all of us are going to die. We can't even keep off death and yet we claim, "Well, we can't take God, we can't believe in God."

No wonder the Bible says, "The fool hath said in his heart there is no God," because a man that would deny the existence of God is a fool.

Most thoughtful people recognize that man is a paradox. He is both dust of earth and breath of God. He is a contradiction of discord and harmony, hatred and love, pride and humility, tolerance and peace and turmoil. The depths to which he sinks only dramatize the heights to which by God's grace he is capable of rising. His very misery is an indication of his potential greatness. His deep yearnings are an echo of what he might be.

When you confess with Isaiah, "I am a man of unclean lips" (Isaiah 6:5), you will stand on the threshold of a victorious life. When you face the fact of your own inadequacy, your own failure, your own sinfulness, you have taken the first step toward gaining a glorious and wonderful personal victory that will carry you through the days of crisis that lie ahead.

It is high time that our so-called experts on marriage, the family and the home turn to the Bible. We have read newspaper columns and listened to counselors on the radio. Psychiatrists have had a land-office business. In it all, the One who performed the first marriage in the Garden of Eden and instituted the union between man and wife has been left out.

The human heart is never a vacuum. If the heart of man is not attuned to God, it becomes a catch basin for every conceivable device of the devil. One of the things Christ warned us against was drunkenness. Alcoholism is one of our most critical problems today.

Alcoholism in the United States is now seven times more prevalent than cancer. The alarming growth of drunkenness cannot be ignored or winked at. To remove moral restraints from society is like taking the bridle off an unbroken horse.

On the newsstands across the country can be bought some of the filthiest literature I have ever seen, completely protected by recent rulings of the Supreme Court. The result is a generation which is surfeiting itself on the appetites of the flesh, to the complete dulling of its spiritual nature and the muting of the voice of conscience. Obsession with sex is evident throughout the length and breadth of the land.

One newspaper columnist commented that more space was given to the love affair of Elizabeth Taylor and Richard Burton than to the combined flights of our five astronauts who risked their lives to bring space travel into realization. Advocates of sex freedom have made a concerted effort to destroy what they term old-fashioned morals. When one considers the forced marriages, the unwed mothers, the growth of venereal disease, our crowded detention homes and our divorce record, one would be willing to admit that they have been successful.

While the world totters on the brink of destruction, millions snore in comfortable complacency and "couldn't care less." With incomes in the United States at an all-time high, we indulge our every whim and purr contentedly like overfed cats. We have forgotten that the price of freedom is eternal vigilance!

When I was in the hospital in Hawaii, I read again of the shocking events which led up to the destruction of the United States fleet at Pearl Harbor. On that fateful day of December 7, 1941, the Japanese attacked. We know now that that attack was invited by our failure to be always vigilant. The result was the destruction of our fleet—the cause was tragic indifference.

. . . When comfort and ease and pleasure are put

ahead of duty and conviction, progress is always set back. What makes us Christians shrug our shoulders when we ought to be flexing our muscles? What makes us apathetic in a day when there are loads to lift, a world to be won and captives to be set free? Why are so many bored when the times demand action? Christ told us that in the last days there would be an insipid attitude toward life.

Modern social righteousness often differs from the righteousness of the Bible. Someone has said, "A wrong deed is right if the majority of people declare it not to be wrong." By this principle we can see our standards shifting from year to year according to the popular vote. Divorce was once frowned upon by society, and laws against fornication and adultery were strictly enforced. But now divorce is accepted by society, fornication is glorified in much of our literature and films, and perversion is looked upon as a biological abnormality rather than a sin.

The same symptoms that were in Rome in its last days are now seen and felt in America. Walk down the streets of our cities and see the names of the films. They are either psychopathic or they are sex, many of them. What is this country coming to? I tell you we need a moral revival. We need a spiritual revival that will put a new moral fiber into our society, or we are done for before the Communists ever get here. We are being softened up right now for the kill. . . . We are being threatened today by racial tension, strife that could bring about cold war between our great races in this country. I want to tell you this: After traveling all over the world I am convinced that one of the greatest black eyes to American prestige abroad is our racial problem in this country. It is high time that we come to the foot of the Cross. When you come to the foot of the Cross and receive Christ as Savior, He gives you the capacity to love your neighbor. I tell you there is no superior race in God's sight. God does not look upon the outward appearance. God looks upon the heart.

Culture is a mollifying ointment rubbed on externally. It cannot reach down to man's deepest need any more than Vaseline can heal cancer. Culture is desirable and commendable, but it is cultivated to the neglect of Christ, it is like putting varnish over a scarred, marred, ugly piece of furniture—it only magnifies the defects.

The divorce rate is as high, or higher, among our so-called cultured groups as it is among the illiterate classes. And as many juvenile delinquents come from homes on the "right" side of the tracks as from the so-called wrong side. It is ironic that thousands of our prison inmates are college graduates and come from the upper bracket of our society. Culture in itself has not kept us from immorality, crime, and the eternal problem of sin; and yet many say . . . "Are not the rivers of culture better than the waters of God?"

A starving man's chief interest is food. A thirsty man's chief interest is water. A wounded man's chief interest is a physician. And a lost man's chief need, whether he realizes it or not, is God.

The trouble with our modern thinking is that we have a conception that God is a haphazard God. He will tell you that every star moves with precision in its celestial path. To ignore the rules of the universe would spell ruin to that star. To deviate from its God-ordained course would mean tragedy and deterioration.

Ask the scientist if God is a haphazard God. He will tell you that his formulas and equations are fixed and that to ignore the laws of science would be a fool's folly. If the laws in the material realm are so fixed and exact, is it reasonable that God could afford to be haphazard in the spiritual realm, where eternal destinies of souls are at stake? I say no, a thousand times no!

God is especially close to us when we are lying on a sickbed. God will make the bed soft and will freshen it with his presence and with his tender care. He makes the bed comfortable and wipes away our tears. He ministers to us with special tenderness at such a time and reveals His great love for us.

Tell me why the gardener trims and prunes his rose-bushes, sometimes cutting away productive branches with both hands, and I will tell you why God's people are afflicted. God's hands never slip. He never makes a mistake. His every move is for our good and for our ultimate good. Oftentimes He must deform us and muti-late our own image. Deformity sometimes precedes con-formity. The knowledge of this caused Paul to sing, "Most gladly therefore will I rather glory in my infir-mities, that the power of Christ may rest upon me."

We have an idea in this country that God is changed to accommodate Himself for Americans. We have an idea that we Americans are God's chosen people, and God loves us more than any other people and that we are God's blessed.

I tell you that God doesn't love us any more than He does the Russians. He doesn't love us any more than he does the Chinese. He doesn't love us any more than he does the Africans. God doesn't love us any more than any other people.

One day I was walking along the road with my little boy, who was then five years of age, and we stepped on an anthill.

We killed a lot of ants and wounded a lot of others, and I said to Ned, "Wouldn't it be wonderful if we could go down there and help those ants rebuild their house and bury their dead, take care of their wounded?"

He said, "But, Daddy, we are too big. We can't get down there and help those ants."

I thought for a moment. "Wouldn't it be wonderful if we could become an ant and live in an ant world?"

And that is what God did. God Almighty decided to become a man and that is who Jesus Christ was.

I believe that Jesus Christ was the most perfectly developed physical specimen in the history of the world. He never had sin to deform his body. His mind was perfect. His nervous system was perfectly coordinated with the rest of his body.

He would have been one of the greatest athletes of all times. Every inch a man.

Over three hundred times the New Testament expresses the fact that Christ is going to come. This has been the hope of the church down through the ages.

It has been called the "blessed hope," the glorious hope that Christ someday will come back to this earth again.

Ladies and gentlemen, on the dark horizon of the present moment I see no other hope. There is really no other possibility I see at the moment for solving the problems of the world than the coming again of Jesus Christ.

The world is darkness and the darkness is growing blacker—frustration, confusion, the world on the horns of a dilemma.

Nature is rife with wonderful examples of new birth —all mysterious and yet wonderful. Take the lowly caterpillar. His lot seems an empty and useless one, threatened by man, beast and fowl. But one day he climbs up into a bush and nature throws a fiber robe around him. He goes to sleep. In a few short weeks there is movement within the fibrous coat, and out of that cocoon emerges a beautiful, resplendent winged creature. He soars over the old pitfalls that used to entrap him, and like a winged angel flies from one fragrant flower to another. A natural metamorphosis? Yes! One which is not easily explained but generally accepted.

The world of nature is filled with beautiful analogies

of the spiritual birth. They all speak eloquently to man, who by nature is given to evil, telling him that there is a higher, more triumphant manner of life for him. The Bible says, "Thou madest him a little lower than the angels; thou crownedst him with glory and honor." (Hebrews 2:7.)

A home is like the solar system. The center, the great sun, holds the solar system together. If it were not for the sun the solar system would fly to pieces. Unless the Son of God is put at the center of your home, it, too, may fly to pieces.

. . . Wherever the cancer of the broken home remains unchecked, this malignant growth eats its way into the vitals of national existence. This is one lesson that stands out with prominence on the pages of world history.

Almost every historian will agree that the disintegration of the Roman Empire was due largely to the broken home. In a recent study of moral conditions in Greece, Persia and Babylonia, the scholars agreed that divorces and broken homes, more than any other single factor, contributed to the downfall of these nations.

Love—I would say physical attraction is the least of it all—is based on congeniality, getting along with each other, liking the same things, doing the same things, and spirituality.

. . . In these modern days the word "father" in some areas has come to mean a character with a highball in one hand, a cigarette in the other, and nothing but sinful mischief in his heart. Thank God, this is true only in a small segment of our society; but unfortunately this idea is growing as fathers take less and less responsibility in the home.

Exercise judgment as to the books you read, the kind of entertainment you attend, the kind of persons with whom you associate. You should no more allow sinful imaginations to accumulate in your mind and soul than you would let garbage accumulate in your living room.

The world is not half so impressed by the things that one does not do as they are by the good things that one does. Certainly, one should not do things that are wrong, but there are thousands of people who glory in what they do not do, while they commit more grievous sins by not doing good things. They are guilty of the sin of omission or of negative living.

A man may not be responsible for his last drink, but he certainly was for the first. No disease germ is powerful enough to lead a man to his first drink. Drinking was a sin first, and a disease last.

. . . Many Christians have been too smug concerning this great and forbidding evil. Negatively they have folded their hands and said: "Drunkenness doesn't bother me," while at the same time they do nothing to "bother drunkenness," and to destroy its devastating power. Christians have often been complacent while such organizations as Alcoholics Anonymous have sprung up to do the job the church should have been doing all the while.

Satan's dream world always ends with disillusionment. Sin, which is his stock and trade, when it is finished brings forth death. There are thousands of people that live in an unreal dream world while shirking their responsibilities toward their family and God. There are thousands of people that read these cheap novels and get a vicarious imaginative thrill out of the experiences they read. There are people that go to the movies or watch television dramas, or listen to soap operas, and then dream that they themselves are living the same type of lives. The Bible calls this "sin." This can become an evil habit that can rob you of the joy of the Lord.

Everybody in the church is for peace. All of us want peace. Everybody wants peace in this nuclear age, but how to achieve peace is not always easy. And you may have peace at the expense of the freedom of millions of people, and there are many moral problems involved here, and I don't think it's just a black-and-white case. It's a complex problem, and . . . the church ought to be praying for the President, for the Secretary of State, for the advisors, that God will lead them to make the right decisions.

We are engaged in this country in a debate on the separation of church and state. It is important that the church and state remain separate, but there is another sense in which Christ cannot be separated from anything that pertains to life, for He "is all, and in all." (Colossians 3:11.) He said, "Ye call me Master and Lord: and . . . so I am." (John 13:13.) He is Master of every phase of our lives.

All through history God has called upon men to take courage. The forces of evil are sweeping through our world today. Lust, greed and hate are manifesting themselves everywhere. Our streets are being turned into asphalt jungles as men rape, mug, rob and kill. Our world stands on the threshold of a nuclear war that could destroy much of civilization. If ever there was a time we needed men and women to mobilize for Jesus Christ, it is now.

Scientists today have come to the point where they are turning to the church to help them for an answer. There is nothing but darkness and blackness as the scientist looks out into the future. He sees the possibility of making a wonderful world. Then he looks into the human heart and realizes that the greatest scientific things of our day are building engines of destruction.

Recently the chairman of one of the most important committees in Congress asked, "Do we need new laws, more streamlined police administration, better law enforcement, heavier sentences or greater funds to curb crime?" Sociologists, psychologists and law-enforcement officers alike are wringing their hands over this situation. They seem to have reached the end of the rope. They do not know what the basic cause is, nor do they know the cure. The basic problem is that we are sinners; and the cure is conversion to Jesus Christ. I'm often accused of oversimplifying these problems, but I believe that we've tried the complex answers too long. It is time to get back to the simplicity and the power of the Gospels to transform individuals as well as society.

One of the problems is that the average person feels that the consistent delinquent, the confirmed criminal or the alcoholic is without hope; so we've often relegated them to the social scrap heap and made little effort to save them. They get lonely, discouraged and burdened with care just as you and I. Remember that within each person beats a heart just like yours. Sin and lawlessness have rushed in to fill the vacuum. When that void is filled with God, the criminal problem is solved for that person.

Personalities are warped by sin; frustration, fears, nervous tension and a thousand and one other psychological problems have gripped millions of Americans because of this moral disease called "sin."

There are no new sins—only new sinners; there are no new crimes—only new criminals; no new evils—only new evildoers; no new pleasures—only new pleasure-seekers. The devil has invented no new gimmicks. Sin and its accompanying effects are now and always have been monotonously the same. The murders you read about are no more shocking or no different from the murder of Abel by Cain; the sex perversions, which our modern newspapers play up as daring and new, are only modern copies of the ancient perversions of Sodom and Gomorrah.

After many thousands of years of so-called progress, education, science and culture, we are annoyed to discover that man is capable of the same old vice and sins, and that as a race we are spiritually little improved.

# BIBLIOGRAPHY

## BOOKS

Adler, Bill. *The Wit and Wisdom of Billy Graham.* New York: Random House, 1967.

Allan, Tom. *Crusade in Scotland.* London: Pickering & Inglis, 1955.

Babbage, Stuart Barton, and Ian Siggins. *Light Beneath the Cross.* Garden City, N.Y.: Doubleday & Company, Inc., 1960.

Bestic, Alan. *Praise the Lord and Pass the Contribution.* New York: Taplinger Publishing Company, 1971.

Burnham, George. *To the Far Corners.* New Jersey: Revell, 1956.

————, and Lee Fisher. *Billy Graham and the New York Crusade.* Grand Rapids: Zondervan Publishing House, 1957.

Colquhoun, Frank. *Harringay Story.* London: Hodder and Stoughton, 1955.

Cook, Charles Thomas. *The Billy Graham Story.* Wheaton, Ill.: Van Kampen Press, 1954.

————. *London Hears Billy Graham.* London: Marshall, Morgan & Scott, 1955.

Gillenson, Lewis W. *Billy Graham and Seven Who Were Saved.* New York: Trident Press, 1967.

Graham, Billy. *The Challenge: Sermons from Madison Square Garden.* Garden City, N.Y.: Doubleday, 1969.

————. *World Aflame*. Garden City, N.Y.: Doubleday and Company, Inc., 1965.

Hall, Gordon Langley. *The Sawdust Trail: the Story of American Evangelism*. Philadelphia: Macrae Smith Company, 1964.

High, Stanley. *Billy Graham: the Personal Story of the Man, His Message, and His Mission*. New York: McGraw-Hill, 1956.

Kilgore, James E. *Billy Graham, the Preacher*. New York: Exposition Press, 1968.

Lockard, W. David. *The Unheard Billy Graham*. Waco, Texas: World Books, 1971.

McLouglin, William G., Jr., *Billy Graham: Revivalist in a Secular Age*. New York: Ronald Press Company, 1960.

Mitchell, Curtis. *Billy Graham: The Making of a Crusader*. Philadelphia and New York: Chilton Books, 1966.

————, *God in the Garden*. Garden City, New York: Doubleday and Company, Inc., 1957.

————. *Those Who Came Forward*. Philadelphia: Chilton Books, 1966.

Morris, James. *The Preachers*. New York: St. Martin's Press, 1973.

Pollock, John Charles. *Billy Graham: The Authorized Biography*. New York: McGraw-Hill Book Company, 1966.

————. *Crusades: 20 Years with Billy Graham*. Minneapolis: World Wide Publications, 1969.

————. *Crusade '66: Britain Hears Billy Graham*. London: Hodder & Stoughton, 1966.

Smart, W. J. *Six Mighty Men*. London: Hodder & Stoughton, 1956.

Streiker, Lowell D., and Gerald S. Strober. *Religion and the New Majority: Billy Graham: Middle America, and the Politics of the 70s*. New York: Association Press, 1972.

Strober, Gerald S. *Graham: A Day in Billy's Life*. New York: Doubleday and Company, Inc., 1976.

PERIODICALS

Barrett, Patricia. "Religion and the 1960 Presidential Election." *Social Order,* June 1962.

Corry, John. "God, Country and Billy Graham." *Harper's Magazine,* February 1969.

Graham, Billy. "Joy of Family Life." *Good Housekeeping,* October 1969.

————. "The Man Called Jesus." *Reader's Digest,* July 1972.

————. "Prayer for a President." *Ladies' Home Journal,* December 1974.

————. "Questions I Am Often Asked." *Reader's Digest,* February 1972.

Hall, Clarence W. "The Charisma of Billy Graham." *Reader's Digest,* July 1970.

Heilman, Joan Rattner. "Billy Graham's Daughter Answers His Critics." *Good Housekeeping,* June 1973.

Henry, Carl F. H. "Evangelicals in the Social Struggle." *Christianity Today,* October 8 1965.

Houston, Noel. "Billy Graham." *Holiday,* February and March 1958.

Lawrence, David. "Billy Graham's Plea to President Johnson." *U.S. News and World Report,* August 7, 1967.

Martin, Harold H. "Revivalist Billy Graham." *Saturday Evening Post,* April 13, 1963.

Palms, Roger C. "Time to Run." *Saturday Evening Post,* August/September 1974.

Raney, Linda, and Joan Gage. "Mrs. Billy Graham: Teaching Children to Believe in God." *Ladies' Home Journal,* December 1972.

Newsmagazines and newspapers, various issues:
*New York Times*
*Time*
*Newsweek*
*U.S. News and World Report*

*Christianity Today*
*The Christian Century*
*The New Yorker*
*London Sunday Times*